German A2

Zeitgeist 2

Teacher's Book

Kirsty Thathapudi
Morag McCrorie
Dagmar Sauer
Maria Hunt

OXFORD
UNIVERSITY PRESS

OXFORD
UNIVERSITY PRESS

Great Clarendon Street, Oxford OX2 6DP

Oxford University Press is a department of the University of Oxford.
It furthers the University's objective of excellence in research, scholarship, and education by publishing worldwide in

Oxford New York

Auckland Cape Town Dar es Salaam Hong Kong Karachi Kuala Lumpur Madrid Melbourne Mexico City Nairobi New Delhi Shanghai Taipei Toronto

With offices in

Argentina Austria Brazil Chile Czech Republic France Greece Guatemala Hungary Italy Japan South Korea Poland Portugal Singapore Switzerland Thailand Turkey Ukraine Vietnam

First published 2009

British Library Cataloguing in Publication Data

Data available

ISBN 978 019 915358 9

10 9 8 7 6 5 4 3 2 1

Typeset by PDQ Digital Media Solutions Ltd., Bungay, Suffolk

Printed in Great Britain by Bell & Bain, Glasgow.

Acknowledgements

The author and publisher would like to thank Kirsty Thathapudi (editor), Melissa Weir (project manager) and Marion Dill (language consultant).

Contents

Symbols used in this Teacher's Book:

Listening material available on CD

S Self-study CD

A 12 Copymaster activities

Extra! Additional extension activities

Summary of unit contents

Unit	Subject content	Grammar	Skills
Einheit 1 Umweltverschmutzung Pollution and energy consumption	Causes and effects of pollution (p.6) Energy consumption and energy supply (p.8) The future of nuclear power (p.10)	Revision of tenses (p.12)	Completing gap-fill activities (pp.7, 12)
Einheit 2 Umweltschutz Conservation of the environment	Recycling (p.16) Conservation of the environment and sustainability (p.18) Sustainability and global responsibility (p.20)	Revision of the passive (pp.17, 22)	Translating from German into English (pp.18, 22, 24)
Wiederholung Einheit 1–2	Revision of Units 1–2 (p.25)		
Einheit 3 Ausländer Immigrants	Who are immigrants? (p.28) Immigrants in Germany (p.30) Racism (p.32)	Using indirect speech (p.34) The subjunctive (p.34)	Translating into German (p.35)
Einheit 4 Armut und Reichtum Poverty and wealth	Poverty in Germany (p.38) The third world (p.40) The fight against poverty (p.42)	Adjective endings (pp.41, 44) Cases (p.44)	Giving opinions (p.45)
Wiederholung Einheit 3–4	Revision of Units 3–4 (p.47)		
Einheit 5 Rechtswesen und Verbrechen Crime and antisocial behaviour	Youth crime (p.50) Internet crime (p.52) Community service, prison or the death penalty (p.54)	Using modal verbs (p.56) The verb *lassen* (p.56) Verbs of perception in the perfect tense (p.56)	Translating into German (pp. 50, 57) Defending a point of view (p.57)
Einheit 6 Technik und die Zukunft The future of technology	Food of the future (p.60) Genetic research (p.62) The technical revolution (p.64)	The imperfect subjunctive (p.65) Using the future perfect (p.66) Using the conditional perfect (p.66)	Improving listening comprehension (p.67)
Wiederholung Einheit 5–6	Revision of Units 5–6 (p.69)		
Einheit 7 Literatur, Film und die bildende Kunst Literature, film and the arts	The joy of reading (p.72) German film today (p.74) Music and painting (p.76)	Using the subjunctive in other ways (p.78)	Research skills (p.79)
Einheit 8 Deutschland heute Germany – past and present	Berlin – the divided city (p.82) Post-reunification Germany (p.84) German-speaking countries and Europe (p.86)	The passive (p.83)	Answering questions in German (p.88)
Wiederholung Einheit 7–8	Revision of Units 7–8 (p.91)		

Unit	Subject content	Grammar	Skills
Einheit 9 Politik – Globale Probleme German and global politics	German and international politics (p.94) Democracy and the power of the individual (p.96) War and terrorism (p.98)	Complex sentence structure using conjunctions (p.100) Using relative pronouns (p.100)	Improving writing (p.101) Selecting appropriate vocabulary for abstract concepts (p.101) Linking sentences grammatically and logically (p.101)
Wiederholung Einheit 9	Revision of Unit 9 (p.103)		
Stretch and Challenge	More demanding activities to reinforce and practise the grammar and skills covered in units 1–9 (pp.105–113)		
Essay-writing skills	Useful advice on producing successful essays (pp. 114–119)		
Grammar	Grammar reference section (p.121)		
Glossary	German–English glossary (p.152)		

Introduction

The course

Welcome to **Zeitgeist 2!**

Zeitgeist 2 is the second stage of a two-part French course written to match the new AS and A2 specifications for AQA, Edexcel, WJEC and CCEA. It has been written by a team of experienced authors and practising teachers and is suitable for a wide range of learners.

Rationale

The aims of **Zeitgeist 2** are:

- to provide thorough coverage of the A2 specifications for AQA, Edexcel, WJEC and CCEA (see grids on pages 11–14 of this book) and prepare students for the A2 examinations
- to provide material suitable for A2 students of all abilities to ease the transition from AS level to A2 level
- to provide comprehensive grammatical coverage and practice of the QCA-defined grammatical content
- to help students develop specific learning strategies, for example dictionary skills, independent study, vocabulary learning and essay-writing techniques
- to enable students to take control of their own learning by means of learning strategies, reference and revision sections, study skills and opportunities for independent study
- to encourage success by providing clear objectives and by practising language via activities with a clear purpose

The components of Zeitgeist 2

Students' Book

The Students' Book is the complete handbook for advanced level studies, providing a comprehensive and integrated programme of teaching, practice, revision and reference for students. This 160-page book contains the following sections:

Einheiten 1–9

There are nine units on different topics. Each unit has been planned to be interesting and motivating, as well as to develop relevant strategies and skills for independent study and preparation for examinations. An outline of the content of each unit is given on Teacher's Book page 4.

Wiederholungen

After every two units, there are two pages with a range of revision activities, aimed at providing further practice and consolidation of the language of the preceding units. Some of the activities are suitable for use in class whereas others are more suitable for homework.

Stretch and Challenge

This section on pages 105–113 of the Students' Book provides students with more demanding activities to reinforce the grammar and skills covered in units 1–9.

Essay-writing skills

This section on pages 114–119 of the Students' Book provides students with useful advice on researching, planning, revising and checking your essay.

Grammatik

This detailed reference section complements the grammar explanations given within the body of the Students' Book. All explanations are in English so that students are able to use this section independently.

Vokabular

This German–English glossary contains many of the words from the Students' Book.

Teacher's Book

Detailed teaching notes for each unit are provided. These notes include:

- suggestions for using the material in the Students' Book, including the revision pages
- answers to most activities, including possible answers where appropriate as well as the correct answers for true/false activities
- transcripts for all recorded material
- notes on when to use the copymasters within each unit
- a sample lesson plan

Oxbox Resource and Assessment CD-Roms

The Oxbox Resource and Assessment CD-Roms provide five copymasters for each unit:

- three general copymasters
- one/two *Prüfungstraining* copymaster(s)
- one/two *Zur Auswahl* copymaster(s)

Assessment material and planning grids are also included on the Oxbox Resource and Assessment CD-Roms.

Grammar Workbook

This 96-page Workbook contains thorough revision and practice of grammar covered in the Students' Book, with an answer booklet for self-marking if appropriate.

Audio CDs

The Audio CDs provide the listening material to accompany the Students' Book. The scripted material was recorded by native German speakers. All CDs may be copied within the purchasing institution for use by teachers and students. The **Zeitgeist Solo** CD is ideal for self-study and it is advisable for students to have an individual copy of this CD to practise independent listening.

CD contents

CD 1: Units 1–5
CD 2: Units 6–9, Stretch and Challenge

Features of a Zeitgeist unit

Unit objectives

Each unit begins with a list of topics with page references to their place in the unit. There are also objectives in English that provide clear information to students about what they will learn in the unit, including grammar and skills. The first page of each unit contains a visual stimulus and some activities to introduce the theme of the unit.

Core spreads

Each of the three core spreads begins with one or two questions to pinpoint what students will learn. Activities in all four skills are included on each spread, leading to a productive spoken or written task at the end of the spread.

Hilfe

These boxes provide key phrases for students to use in their written and spoken outcome tasks.

Grammatik

Grammatik sections focus on a key grammar point. The explanations and instructions in these sections are in English, enabling students to use them independently. Activities are provided (lettered A, B, C, etc.) to reinforce each grammar point, and examples are included in texts on the spread so that students have an opportunity to see the grammar point in practice. There are also cross-references to pages in the grammar reference section and the Grammar Workbook.

Tipp

These sections provide practical skills advice and language-learning tips in English, with activities (lettered A, B, C, etc.) enabling students to put the advice into practice. They are ideal for self-study and are intended to improve aspects of students' performance and help them develop as independent learners.

Extra!

These are additional activities, often provided on a copymaster, to extend what students have learnt on the spread.

Prüfungstraining

These two exam-practice pages provide students with additional activities to practise and improve the grammar, skills and examination techniques of the unit.

Zur Auswahl

At the end of each unit there is a page of self-study activities to reinforce the language, skills and grammar that students have learnt in the unit. The listening activities are recorded on a self-study CD.

Wiederholungen

These sections provide revision practice with exam-style questions to help students prepare for their A2 examination.

Zeitgeist and the new AS and A2 specifications

Zeitgeist is a structured two-part course intended for use over two years' study and has been written to follow the revised AS/A2 specifications for AQA, Edexcel, WJEC and CCEA. There are nine units in **Zeitgeist 2**, written to match the content of the revised A2 specifications. The style and content of the activities would also be appropriate for use with other exam specifications.

Grammar

Zeitgeist 2 provides complete coverage of the QCA-defined grammar content. The deductive approach on the Students' Book pages and the extensive practice provided in the Grammar Workbook ensure that students are able to master all aspects of language structure required at this level.

Assessment

The assessment material in **Zeitgeist 2** has been written to match the style of the major examination boards. Practice in tackling exam-style questions is provided on the Oxbox Resource and Assessment CD-Roms. Mark schemes for the assessments are provided in the teaching notes that are included on the Oxbox Resource and Assessment CD-Roms.

Key skills

The table below provides an overview of key skills coverage in **Zeitgeist 2**. It shows where there are opportunities to develop and/or assess some or all of the criteria for each key skill at level 3.

The following notes provide examples of how each key skill may be developed or assessed through the activities in **Zeitgeist 2**:

Communication

Teachers should note that, although the study of a modern foreign language helps students to develop their communication skills, *the evidence for this Key Skill must be presented in English, Irish or Welsh.* **Zeitgeist 2** offers opportunities for practising and developing communication skills rather than for generating assessed evidence.

For this key skill, students need to:

1a Take part in a group discussion
All **Zeitgeist 2** units provide opportunities for students to discuss topics in pairs, small groups or as whole-class activity.

1b Make a formal presentation of at least eight minutes
Many of the topics covered in the coursebook provide a suitable basis for a presentation. Students should be encouraged to support their presentations using visuals (e.g. OHP transparencies, photographs, brochures, etc.), PowerPoint, audio clips and other appropriate material.

2 Read and synthesize information from at least two documents about the same subject
Zeitgeist 2 provides reading material on a wide range of topics, with activities designed to help students identify main points and summarize information. Students are also encouraged to undertake wider reading when researching information for productive spoken and written work. Their wider reading might include newspapers, magazines, books, publicity material, and Internet sources.

3 Write two different types of document
Opportunities exist throughout **Zeitgeist 2** for students to attempt extended writing in a variety of styles, e.g. reports, essays and creative material on a wide range of themes, a biography, publicity material, informal and formal letters, etc.

Application of number

Although it may not be within the scope of a modern foreign language course to generate sufficient evidence to assess this key skill, **Zeitgeist 2** does provide opportunities for students to develop their ability to work with numbers. Numbers feature in most units (e.g. dates/years, percentages, statistics, population figures, etc.); however, the table above indicates only those units where students are involved in interpreting or commenting on statistics.

Information and communications technology

Students need to be able to:

1 search for and select information
2 enter and develop the information, and derive new information
3 present combined information such as text with image, text with number, image with number

Many **Zeitgeist 2** units provide opportunities for students to develop aspects of this key skill. Criteria 1–3 (listed above) can be combined in a single extended piece of work in activities such as the following:

		1	2	3	4	5	6	7	8	9
Main key skills	*Communication*	✓	✓	✓	✓	✓	✓	✓	✓	✓
	Application of number	✓		✓		✓				
	ICT	✓	✓		✓	✓		✓	✓	✓
Wider key skills	*Working with others*	✓	✓	✓	✓	✓	✓	✓	✓	✓
	Improving own learning and performance	✓	✓	✓	✓	✓	✓	✓	✓	✓
	Problem solving	✓	✓	✓	✓	✓	✓	✓	✓	✓

- Unit 5, page 51, activity 6: Students prepare a presentation on the topic of youth crime.
- Unit 9, page 93, activity 2b: Students use the Internet to research German politics, using the photos in the Students' Book as a starting point. They then give a one-minute presentation to the rest of the class, for which they could use visual stimuli, produced using desktop publishing.

Working with others
All **Zeitgeist 2** units provide opportunities for students to work together, either in a one-to-one situation or as part of a group. These opportunities may take the form of interviews, discussions, debates and surveys, or they may involve students in a more creative activity such as inventing a role-play.

The following example shows how a group task can be developed and expanded in order to become a suitable means of assessing this key skill:

Unit 5, page 55, activities 3a and 3b: Students work with a partner to discuss the advantages and disadvantages of 'brat camps'. They then discuss this topic as a class.

1. They begin by dividing into pairs and preparing arguments for and against 'brat camps'.
2. Once they have prepared their arguments, they conduct the debate, using the *Hilfe* phrases and the guidance provided in the *Tipp* on page 57. The *Tipp* will aid them in defending their point of view.
3. After completion of the task, students can review their work, sharing constructive feedback and agreeing on ways to improve collaborative work in future.

Improving own learning and performance
Students are required to:

1. set targets and plan how these will be met
2. take responsibility for own learning and use plans to help meet targets and improve performance
3. review progress and establish evidence of achievements

All **Zeitgeist 2** units provide opportunities to meet these criteria through:

- **Clear objectives and means of reviewing progress**
  Each unit begins with a list of objectives, providing clear information to students about what they will learn in the unit, including grammar and skills. In addition to these unit objectives, students should be encouraged to set their own personal targets relating to aspects of their performance that they want to improve, with an action plan showing how they intend to achieve the targets and how they will assess their progress. The *Wiederholung* sections at the end of each couple of units provide students with a means of reviewing their progress.
- **Strategies for improving performance**
  All **Zeitgeist 2** units include *Tipp* sections, which suggest strategies and activities to help students develop as independent learners and improve aspects of their own performance. Strategies range from specific listening, speaking, reading and writing advice to tips on using dictionaries effectively and suggestions on recording and learning new language.

Problem solving
Although a modern foreign language course may not generate sufficient evidence to assess this key skill, language learning does provide opportunities to practise and develop problem-solving skills. For example, a 'problem' in language learning can take the form of any unknown word or phrase. If students are encouraged to 'work out' new language for themselves and take responsibility for their own learning instead of relying on teacher support, they develop problem-solving skills.

All **Zeitgeist 2** units provide opportunities for students to do this. In particular, the *Tipp* sections encourage students to become more independent in their language learning.

Information and communications technology

These notes provide a few examples of ways to use ICT with **Zeitgeist**. For more detailed information on current software and technologies, together with practical help and ideas on the use of ICT in the modern foreign languages classroom, you may find the following helpful:

- Becta (British Educational Communications and Technology Agency)
  www.becta.org.uk
- CILT (The National Centre for Languages)
  www.cilt.org.uk
- Languages ICT
  www.languages-ict.org.uk

Internet
Note on Internet safety: Before using the Internet with students, whether for online communication,

the creation of web pages and blogs, or for research purposes, it is vital to be aware of safety issues. Guidance on this can be obtained from Becta (see website above).

Online communication

If your school has links with a partner school in a German-speaking country, the Internet offers a range of ways in which your students can communicate with their German counterparts, e.g. email, instant messaging, chat rooms, noticeboards and forums, audio- and video-conferencing, web pages and blogs. These enable the exchange of a wide range of information, from text and graphics to audio and video clips. They are extremely useful for motivating students, encouraging spontaneous communication and generating a source of additional teaching and learning material.

Internet research

The Internet can be a valuable research tool, giving both teachers and students easy access to authentic reading materials and cultural information about German-speaking countries. Opportunities for students to research on the Internet occur throughout **Zeitgeist**. Themes include:

- Unit 2, page 24, activity 1c: ecologically-sound living
- Unit 4, page 43, activity 5: German charities
- Unit 7, page 75, activity 5: German film
- Unit 8, page 89, activity 4: German festivals
- Unit 9, page 93, activity 2b: German politics

Word-processing and text manipulation

Word-processing software allows text to be presented in a variety of forms that can be easily edited and manipulated. This makes it easier for students to experiment with language and to draft and redraft their work. Any written task can be completed on the computer, e.g.

- Unit 1, page 11, activity 6: Students write a letter to a newspaper on the danger of nuclear energy or on nuclear energy being safer in the future.
- Unit 4, page 39, activity 5: Students imagine they are homeless and write an article for the newspaper BISS.
- Unit 7, page 73, activity 5: Students write a passage summarising the life and work of an author.
- Unit 8, page 85, activity 6: Students play the part of an *Ossi* and write a letter to relatives in the former West Germany, describing how their life has changed since the fall of the Berlin wall.

Desktop publishing

Desktop publishing software enables students to design sophisticated documents involving complex layout of text, clip art, digital photos and scanned images, e.g. brochures, posters and articles. Opportunities for students to use desktop publishing in **Zeitgeist** include:

- Unit 8, page 89, activity 5: Students imagine they have been to a German festival and write up a report about the event.
- Unit 9, page 97, activity 4b: Students design a poster advertising a chosen cause.

Databases and spreadsheets

Data-processing software allows text- and number-based information gathered by students, possibly during a class survey, to be entered into a database then sorted and analysed in different ways; spreadsheet software is more suitable for dealing with number-based (rather than text-based) data. Both of these technologies generate a range of opportunities for further language work, comparison and discussion of the data, etc.

Opportunities to use these technologies in **Zeitgeist** include:

- Unit 2, page 24, activity 4: After students have ranked the environmental problems in what they consider to be the order of importance, they could compile a database and discuss the results.

Presentation software

Presentation software (e.g. PowerPoint) allows students to create multimedia 'slides' combining text, images, sound and video clips, active links to web pages, animations, etc. The slides can be displayed to the whole class via a data projector and wall screen or interactive whiteboard. Themes for oral presentations in **Zeitgeist** include:

- Unit 5, page 51, activity 6: Students prepare a presentation on the topic of youth crime.

AQA Specification Match

AQA topics and sub-topics (A2 Level)	Zeitgeist 2 Students' Book reference
Environment	
Pollution	
Types, causes and effects of pollution	Unit 1 pp6–7: climate change, greenhouse effect
Measures to reduce pollution	Unit 1 pp8–9: eco-friendly house building
Individual action-responsibility	Unit 2 pp15–17: recycling, responsible use of product
Transport issues	Unit 1 p5: alternative solutions, e.g. electric car *Stretch & Challenge* p105: energy 'ID card' for property *Stretch & Challenge* p106 aviation/railway and pollution
Energy	
Coal, oil and gas	Unit 1 p8: statistics on worldwide consumption
Nuclear	Unit 1 pp10–11: cases for and against nuclear energy
Alternative energy sources	Unit 1 p14: wind energy Unit 1 p14: location of wind turbines
Changing attitudes to energy consumption	Unit 1 pp8–9: eco-friendly architecture *Stretch & Challenge* p105: energy 'ID card' for property
Protecting the planet	
Ways of minimising environmental damage	Unit 2 pp15–17: responsible recycling Unit 1 pp8–9: eco-friendly house building
The role of pressure groups	Unit 2 pp18–19: Greenpeace protest
Initiatives to improve awareness and change behaviour	Unit 1 p14: development of the first wind turbine
Responsibilities towards other nations, especially developing countries	Unit 2 pp20–21: principles of global sustainability Unit 2 pp20–21: climate change & environmental effects worldwide: desecration of tropical rain forest/deserts
The Multicultural Society	
Immigration	
Reasons for immigration	Unit 3 pp27–29: asylum seekers, *Gastarbeiter*
Benefits and problems of immigration for immigrants & for country of destination	Unit 3 pp30–31: comparative immigrants' experiences
Migration within the enlarged EU	Unit 3 pp28–29: immigrants from Eastern European states
Curbs on immigration	Unit 3 p28: restrictions in Germany *Stretch and challenge* p107: need for skilled workers Unit 3 pp28–29:asylum application and regulation
Integration	
Factors making integration difficult	Unit 2 pp30–31: three immigrants' experiences: language, unemployment
Factors facilitating integration	Unit 2 p28: East European immigrants with German heritage
To which culture should immigrants show loyalty?	Unit 3 pp30–31: generational differences in attitude
Experiences of individual immigrants	Unit 3 pp28–29: European and wider world migrant workers and asylum seekers Unit 3 pp30–31: asylum seeker, *Gastarbeiter*, migrant worker perspectives *Stretch & Challenge* p107: specific employment difficulties
Racism	
Victims of racism & reasons for racism	Unit 3 pp32–33: victims of racially motivated crime
Measures to eliminate racism and their effectiveness	Unit 3 pp34–35: school anti-racism forum
Experiences of individuals, including those of 2nd or 3rd generation immigrants	Unit 3 pp30–31: asylum seeker, migrant worker, guest worker Unit 3 pp32–33: victims of racially motivated crime
Wealth and poverty	

Contemporary Social Issues	
Causes of poverty in Europe and developing countries	Unit 4 pp38–39, p46: child poverty, family problems in Germany *Stretch & Challenge* p108: children at risk Unit 4 pp40–41: war, over-population, etc. in developing countries
Work of charitable organisations and governments	Unit 4 pp42–43: Fairtrade aid Unit 4 pp44–45: medical aid Unit 4 p46: child protection agencies
Attitudes to wealth and poverty; link between wealth and poverty	Unit 4 pp38–39: comparative statistics Unit 4 p46: attitudes towards 3rd world poverty & child protection agencies
Law and order	
Examples of crime, especially committed by or affecting young people	Unit 5 pp50–51: comparative statistics 1998 & 2006 Unit 5 pp52–53: growth of Internet crime
Reasons for criminal and anti-social behaviour	Unit 5 pp49–51: social environment, abuse, drugs *Stretch & Challenge* p109: reasons and solutions
Measures to reduce crime and their effectiveness	Unit 5 p58: surveillance, e.g. CCTV – for and against
Alternatives to imprisonment, their appropriateness and effectiveness	Unit 5 pp54–55: debate – boot camps, prison or death penalty Unit 5 pp56–57: re-education, recognition of crime, perpetrators' own solutions
Impact of scientific and technological progress	
Technology in the home and workplace, including IT	Unit 6 p59, pp64–65, p68: work place robots, picture phones, 100% domestic access to Internet *Stretch & Challenge* p110: Internet shopping
Space and satellite technology Medical research	Unit 6 p59: life in space
Ethical issues linked to scientific and technological progress	Unit 6 pp60–61, p69: genetic modification of food, genetic research & human cloning stem cell Unit 6 pp64–65: employment affected/ jeopardised by IT Unit 6 pp62–63, pp66–67: human genetic medical research & cloning Unit 6 p68: protection of endangered animals
Cultural Topic	
A target language-speaking region/community	Unit 8 p81: fact find: population, geographical features, etc. Unit 8 pp82–83: Berlin Unit 8 pp84–85: former DDR Unit 8 pp86–87: effect of the Euro Unit 8 pp88–89: festivals – München, Berlin Unit 9 pp96–97: Rheinsberg *'Kulturhauptstadt'*
A period of 20th century history from a target language-speaking country/community	Unit 8 pp82–83: Berlin 1961–1989 Unit 8 pp84–85, Unit 9 pp100–101: changes since reunification Unit 8 pp86–87: 2002–present day – effect of the Euro Unit 8 p90: opening of EU borders Unit 9 pp98–99: war and terrorism in 20th and 21st centuries Unit 9 pp96–97: present day democracy Unit 9 pp102–104: Parliament and party politics *Stretch & Challenge* p112: Berlin Air Blockade
The work of an author from a target language- speaking country/community	Unit 7 p71: various authors Unit 7 pp72–73: Julia Franck & Katharina Hacker *Wiederholung* 7–8 p91: online publishing
The work of a director, architect, musician or painter from a target language- speaking country/community	Unit 7 p71: various directors & musicians Unit 7 pp74–75: Films from 1970s–21st century *Wiederholung* 7–8 p92: Film – *Das Leben der Anderen* Unit 7 pp76–77: successful German band *Tokio Hotel*; artist Gustav Klimt

Edexcel Specification Match

Topics and Sub-topics (A2 Level)	Zeitgeist 2 Students' book reference
Customs, traditions, beliefs and religions	
Festivals	Unit 8 pp88–89: Oktoberfest, Fasching/Karneval, Berliner Love-Parade
National and International events: past present and future	
(Environment)	(Unit 1 p14: establishment of first wind turbine)
History	Unit 8 pp82–83: 1961–1989 a divided Berlin Unit 8 pp84–85: Germany since 1989 Unit 8 pp86–87: introduction of the Euro
Science	Unit 6 pp60–61: introduction of genetically modified foodstuffs
Literature and the Arts	
Literature	Unit 7 p71: short book resumés Unit 7 pp72–73: famous writers: Goethe,Brecht & Böll. New authors Julia Franck & Katharina Hecker *Wiederholung* 7–8 p91: online publishing
Film	Unit 7 p71: short film resumés Unit 7 pp74–75: film from 1970s into the 21st century including *Berlin Alexanderplatz* and *Der Untergang* *Wiederholung* 7–8 p92: resumé of *Das Leben der Anderen*
Art	Unit 7 pp76–77: Gustav Klimt
Music	Unit 7 p71: short notes on contemporary bands, Unit 7 pp76–77: German band *Tokio Hotel*
Research-based essay	
Geographical area	Unit 8 p81: German-speaking countries
Historical study	Unit 8 pp82–83: Berlin 1961–1989 Unit 8 pp84–85: Germany since reunification Unit 8 pp86–87: economic and political role of German-speaking countries in Europe Unit 8 p90: future role of EU Unit 9 pp96–97: democratic rights, protest, direct action Unit 9 pp98–99: war and terrorism 20th-21st century Unit 9 pp102–103: parliament and party politics
Aspects of modern German-speaking society	
Environment	Unit 1 pp8–9: eco-friendly house building Unit 1 pp10–11: nuclear energy Unit 1 p14: establishment of wind turbines Unit 2 pp24–25: eco-friendly office & solar energy
Immigration & Racism	Unit 3 pp28–29: *Gastarbeiter*, asylum seekers, immigrants & nomadic workers Unit 3 pp30–31: individual experiences of immigrant workers Unit 3 pp32–34: racism: reasons and consequences Unit 3 pp34-35: establishment of school anti-racism forum
Poverty and Wealth	Unit 4 pp38–39: child & family poverty – reasons and consequences Unit 4 pp44–45: German aid to third world
Crime & Justice	Unit 5 pp50–51: analysis of youth crime Unit 5 pp52–53: Internet crime Unit 5 pp54–55: comparative penal systems: boot camp, prison, etc.
Technology	Unit 6 p59, pp64–65, p68: work place robots, picture phones, 100% domestic access to the Internet *Stretch and challenge* p110: Internet shopping Unit 6 p59 life in space Unit 6 pp64–65: employment jeopardised by IT
Medical and ethical issues	Unit 6 pp60–61, p69: genetic modification of food, genetic research and human cloning pp68–69 protection of endangered animals through genetic research and experimentation

WJEC Specification Match

Environmental issues	
Technology pollution	Unit 1 pp6–7: causes and effects: toxic emissions, greenhouse effect. etc.
Global warming	Unit 1 pp6–7: climate change, greenhouse effect Unit 1 p13: effect on alpine environment Unit 2 pp20–21: political initiatives and solutions
Transport	Unit 1 p5: comparative transport problems *Stretch and Challenge* p106: environmental damages caused by aviation compared with car/rail
Energy	Unit 1 p8: statistics on global and EU energy use and need
Nuclear energy	Unit 1 pp10–11: arguments for and against
Renewable energies	Unit 1 p14: development of wind turbines Unit 1 pp8–9: eco-friendly house building Unit 2 p25: solar energy in southern Europe
Conservation	Unit 2 pp18–19: Greenpeace initiatives Unit 2 pp20–21: protection of global eco-system: tropical rain forest, endangered species
Recycling	Unit 2 pp15–17: effectiveness of recycling programmes Unit 2 p23: national and global recycling targets
Sustainability	*Stretch and Challenge* p105: energy 'ID' card for property Unit 2 p24: eco-friendly office
Social and political issues	
Role of the media	—
Racism	Unit 3 pp32–33: right-wing extremism and violence Unit 3 pp34–35: school anti-racist forum Unit 9 pp96–97: anti-nazi people's initiative
Immigration	Unit 3 pp28–31: asylum seekers, migrant workers, *Gastarbeiter* Unit 3 p36: young people's initiatives
Social exclusion	Unit 3 pp27–31: problems of immigrant workers Unit 3 p34: extremist action
Integration	Unit 3 p36: young people's integration initiatives Unit 3 pp34–35: school anti-racist forum
Terrorism	Unit 9 p99: terrorist atrocities: 9/11, London July 2006, Madrid station 2004, etc.
World of work (employment, commerce, globalisation, etc.)	Unit 8 pp84–85: employment changes since reunification Unit 8 pp86–87: role of German speaking countries in Europe: economy, industry and employment Unit 8 p90: German/French relationship within the EU *Stretch and Challenge* p113: unions and strike action

CCEA Specification Match

Local and Global Citizenship	
Equality and inequality – types/causes	Unit 3 pp27–31: difficulties for migrant workers, asylum seekers: unequal pay, limitations on employment, language barriers
Achieving equality in society	Unit 3 pp30–31: immigrant perspectives on attaining equality
Discrimination and prejudice – causes and consequences	Unit 3 pp32–33: racism against immigrant workers: low paid work, victims of crime
Dealing with discrimination and prejudice	Unit 3 pp34–35: school anti-racism forum Unit 3 p36: international support café for asylum seekers
Poverty – causes and consequences	Unit 4 pp37–39, p46: child & family poverty in Germany Unit 4 pp40–41: war, overpopulation, lack of medical provision in developing countries
Eradicating poverty locally and globally	Unit 4 pp38–39: homelessness: proactive self support Unit 4 pp42–43: Third World aid & support: Fairtrade Unit 4 pp44–45: Western medical aid in Malawi *Stretch & Challenge* pp108–109 care of children & young people at risk
Multicultural society – challenges and pressures	Unit 3 pp27–29: immigrant workers, asylum seekers' personal perspectives Unit 3 pp32–33: racial extremism and anti-racist initiatives Unit 3 p36: community initiatives: café and homework club
Recent developments and changes	Unit 3 pp34–35: school anti-racism forum Unit 3 p36: international support cafe for asylum seekers
Immigration- issues, benefits, integration	Unit 3 pp27–29: asylum seekers, emigrant workers, *Gastarbeiter*
Understanding cultural differences	Unit 3 pp30–31: female perspective Unit 3 pp34–35: school anti-racism forum Unit 3 p36 international support café
Development of local and global democracy	Unit 9 pp96–97: the right to demonstrate Unit 9 pp100–101: party politics since 1989 Unit 9 p102: reduction of voting age *Stretch and Challenge* p113: consequences of strike action
Causes and consequences of conflict and ending conflict	Unit 8 pp82–83: post war Berlin Unit 9 p98: German perspective of war Unit 9 p99: terrorist atrocities: 9/11, London July 2006
Environmental Awareness	
Importance of conservation for society	Unit 2 pp18–19: Greenpeace campaigns Unit 2 pp20–21: global initiatives
Different types of conservation	Unit 2 pp18–19: Greenpeace campaigns
Opposition to conservation	—
Pollution and waste – sources and solutions	Unit 1 pp5–7: global warming, climate change, industrial pollution
Alternative and renewable energy sources	Unit 1 pp8–9: eco-friendly house building Unit 1 pp10–11: nuclear energy pros & cons *Wiederholung* 1–2 p25: solar power in building
Causes and consequences of climate change	Unit 1 pp6–7: industrial incineration, CO^2 emissions, greenhouse effect Unit 1 p13: climate change in Germany *Stretch and Challenge* p106: CO^2 aviation emissions
Role of governments in protecting the environment	Unit 1 pp10–11: nuclear energy programmes Unit 1 p14: development & establishment of wind turbine
Collective and personal responsibility	Unit 2 pp15–17: recycling: industrial and domestic *Stretch and Challenge* p105: 'Energy Passport' for house owners

Lesson Plan

<table>
<tr><td colspan="2">Date:</td><td colspan="2">Teacher:</td><td colspan="2">Class:</td></tr>
<tr><td colspan="3">Objectives</td><td colspan="3">Resources</td></tr>
<tr><td colspan="3"></td><td colspan="3"></td></tr>
<tr><td colspan="3">Objectives for Students</td><td colspan="3">Notes/Reminders</td></tr>
<tr><td colspan="3"></td><td colspan="3"></td></tr>
<tr><td colspan="6">Starter:</td></tr>
<tr><td colspan="6">Teaching sequence:</td></tr>
<tr><td colspan="6">Differentiation/Extension:</td></tr>
<tr><td colspan="6">Plenary:</td></tr>
<tr><td colspan="6">Homework:</td></tr>
</table>

Umweltverschmutzung Einheit 1

Unit objectives

By the end of this unit students will be able to:

- Discuss the causes and effects of pollution
- Suggest measures to reduce pollution
- Discuss the issue of individual versus collective responsibility
- Discuss pros and cons of fossil versus renewable energy sources

Grammar

By the end of this unit students will be able to:

- Use tenses

Skills

By the end of this unit students will be able to:

- Complete gap-fill activities

Materials

- Students' Book page 5

1a As an introduction, students match the captions to the pictures.

Answers:
1 c **2** i **3** a **4** f **5** b **6** h **7** j **8** e **9** g **10** d

1b Students work in pairs to decide to match the solutions with each of the problems listed. They then discuss other possible solutions to these problems.

1c Students discuss with a partner what they think is the biggest environmental problem and why. Encourage them to draw upon ideas from lb.

Ursachen und Auswirkungen

Skills focus

- Gap-fill exercises

Materials

- Students' Book pages 6–7
- CD 1, track 2
- *Arbeitsblätter* 1,2

1 Students look at six photos and decide what they have in common.

2a Students match the German to the appropriate English translation.

Answers:
1 e **2** a **3** d **4** f **5** b **6** c

2b/c Students read the text and make a list of the causes and effects of pollution mentioned.

Answers:
Causes: *burning/incinerating, traffic, CO_2 emissions from coal, natural gases and oil*
Effects: *Greenhouse effect, global warming, rising sea temperatures, species of animals and plants becoming extinct, ice ages, more storm tides, hurricanes, heat waves, torrential rain, an increase in tropical cyclones*

3 Students complete the sentences with the correct word from the box. Point out that there are more words than gaps.

Answers:
a *Verkehr*
b *Brennstoffe*
c *Erwärmung*
d *Anpassung*
e *Fabriken, Energie*

4a Students look up the list of words in a dictionary.

4b Students listen to the discussion about climate change and decide whether each sentence is true (R), false (F) or not mentioned (N).

Answers:
a F **b** N **c** R **d** N **e** R

p 7, activities 4b and 4c

Andreas: Also, Claudia, was meinst Du? Kann man den Klimawandel überhaupt verhindern?

Claudia: Ganz verhindern kann man ihn wohl nicht, aber bremsen beziehungsweise verlangsamen. Wir müssen auf jeden Fall die CO_2-Emissionen reduzieren – das heißt, also weniger fossile Energieträger wie Kohle oder Öl verbrennen. Wenn man alternative Energien wie Windkraft, Solarenergie oder Wasserkraft benutzt, kann man die Treibhausgase verringern. Was meinst du, Andreas?

Andreas: Ich finde auch, dass die Entwicklung neuer Technologien sehr wichtig ist. Zum Beispiel könnten Autos mit Wasserstoff fahren, bei denen Wasserstoff das Benzin ersetzen würde. Man muss allerdings den Wasserstoff mit Hilfe alternativer Energien produzieren, denn sonst

	würde ein Auto, das mit Wasserstoff fährt, vielleicht sogar mehr Emissionen freisetzen. Aber ganz auf das Auto zu verzichten möchte ich eigentlich nicht. Findest du nicht, Susi?
Susi:	Du könntest aber mit dem Rad fahren oder öffentliche Verkehrsmittel benutzen. Aber es gibt noch andere Treibhausgase außer CO_2. Schau dir zum Beispiel die Mülldeponien an. Sie setzen ein Treibhausgas frei, und wenn man das auffängt und es als Brennstoff benutzt, kann man sogar Wärme daraus gewinnen.
Andreas:	Ja, das habe ich auch schon gehört. Außerdem sollte man die Wälder nicht abholzen. Das ist besonders in tropischen Ländern ein Problem, weil man dort das Land dann für Weideland benutzt. Stimmst du mir da nicht zu, Claudia?
Claudia:	Abholzen trägt nicht immer zum Klimawandel bei. Wenn man Holz benutzt, um Energie zu produzieren, gelangt zwar Kohlenstoff in die Atmosphäre, aber wenn man neue Bäume dort pflanzt, wo man die alten abgeholzt hat, nehmen die neuen Bäume das Kohlendioxid aus der Atmosphäre auf, und es wird ein Kreislauf hergestellt. Das ist jedoch ein langer und nicht besonders effizienter Prozess. Brennstoffe aus Biomasse herzustellen ist deshalb nicht die beste Möglichkeit.

4c Students listen to the discussion again and note down the main points.

5a As a class, students discuss how best to slow down climate change. What do they do to help?

5b As a class, record the conclusion of the discussion from activity 5a in written form.

Energieverbrauch und –versorgung

Materials

- Students' Book pages 8–9
- CD 1, track 3
- *Arbeitsblatt* 3

1 Students compare the two pie-charts and think about how Germany's energy consumption could look.

2a Students match the sentences.

Answers:
a 4 b 7 c 1 d 6 e 2 f 3 g 5

2b Students listen to a report about energy supply in Germany and complete the sentences with the correct figure.

Answers:

a *Der Energieverbrauch ist seit den 70er Jahren um **50%** gestiegen.*

b *In der Zukunft soll der Energieverbrauch um **8%** zurückgehen.*

c *Die größten Anteile an der Energieversorgung haben Mineralöl mit **37%** und Erdgas mit **23%**.*

d *Die Bundesregierung will **40 Milliarden** Euro in erneuerbare Energien investieren.*

e *Bis zum Jahr **2020** sollen **10%** des Stromverbrauchs durch erneuerbare Energien gedeckt werden.*

f *Die Renovierung von Gebäuden will die Bundesregierung mit **1,4 Milliarden** Euro unterstützen.*

p 8, activity 2b

Während sich der Energieverbrauch seit den 70er Jahren weltweit fast verdoppelt hat, ist der Energieverbrauch in Deutschland schon jahrelang ziemlich stabil. Im Jahr 2005 lag er um 4,5% unter dem Wert von 1990. Man erwartet, dass der Energieverbrauch pro Einwohner bis zum Jahr 2020 um weitere 8% sinken wird.

Im Jahr 2005 lag der Anteil an Mineralöl bei ungefähr 37% und der Anteil an Erdgas bei 23%. Kohle trägt mit 24% und die erneuerbaren Energiequellen tragen mit rund 4,7% zur Energieversorgung bei. Der Anteil der Kernenergie lag bei zirka 12%.

Die Bundesregierung will die Verbraucher und Unternehmen weiterhin zum Energiesparen und zur effizienteren Energienutzung anregen, denn die Bundesregierung hat sich ehrgeizige Ziele gesetzt. 40 Milliarden Euro sind für die Weiterentwicklung von erneuerbaren Energien geplant. Der Anteil an erneuerbaren Energiequellen am gesamten Stromverbrauch soll bis 2020 10% betragen. Außerdem will die Regierung mehr Geld in die Energieforschung investieren sowie eine Gebäudesanierung mit 1,4 Milliarden Euro fördern. Da es sich bei der Energieversorgung um ein globales Thema
handelt, hält die Bundesregierung eine eurpäische und internationale Zusammenarbeit für sehr wichtig.

(www.bundesregierung.de – Energieversorgung)

3a Students read the text, *Energiesparen durch Niedrigbauweise und Passivhäuser.*

3b Students complete the sentences in accordance with the reading text.

Answers:
a 3 **b** 2 **c** 2 **d** 1

3c Students answer the questions in full sentences.

4 Students translate the sentences into German.

Answers:
- **a** *Passivhäuser sind umweltfreundlicher, aber teurer als konventionelle Wohnbauten.*
- **b** *Langfristig lohnt es sich, mehr zu bezahlen, um Energie zu sparen.*
- **c** *Passivhäuser sind dreifach verglast und brauchen keine Heizung, weil die Wärme im Haus gespeichert wird.*

5 Students work in pairs. One tries to persuade the other to build a *Passivhaus*. Encourage them to use the vocabulary and ideas presented in the reading text in their discussion.

6 Students write a short passage summarising what German people are doing to safeguard energy supply for the future and express their opinion. They should also mention what they are doing to help. Encourage them to use the vocabulary and ideas presented on pages 8 and 9 of the Students' Book in their writing.

Mit Atomenergie in die Zukunft?

Materials

- Students' Book pages 10–11
- CD 1, track 4

1 Students read the opinions of the two young people. With which do they agree and why? They discuss this in pairs.

2a Students read the interview with Herr Müller, who is opposed to nuclear power.

2b Students match the phrases with the definitions.

Answers:
a 4 **b** 3 **c** 5 **d** 7 **e** 6 **f** 1 **g** 2

2c Students read the sentences and choose the best verb to fit each gap.

Answers:
- **a** *Wenn Deutschland aus der Atomenergie **aussteigt**, muss das Land andere Energiequellen **benutzen**.*
- **b** *Viele Einwohner **stehen** der Atomenergie skeptisch **gegenüber**.*
- **c** *Die Bundesregierung **will** in neue Kohlekraftwerke investieren.*
- **d** *In England **ersetzt** man die alten Atomreaktoren.*
- **e** *Es ist wichtig, dass die Regierung die Energieversorgung in der Zukunft **gewährleistet.***
- **f** *In Deutschland will man erneuerbare Technologien **fördern**.*

3a Students look up the words in the box in a dictionary.

Answers:
nachhaltig = lasting, for a long time
Lebensunterhalt = one's living
beweisen = to prove

3b Students listen to the discussion between a supporter of and an opponent of the nuclear industry and note down:
- arguments for nuclear power
- arguments against nuclear power
- the situation in other countries

Answers:
For: *Meets energy needs; clean and efficient; provides employment in power plants*

Against: *Should tap into alternative energy sources such as solar power – although these are more expensive at the moment, they are lasting and safer; these energy sources provide jobs and don't know exactly what the health risks are of working in or living close to a nuclear power plant (e.g. could increase risk of cancer); danger of nuclear waste*

Other countries: *France has 50 nuclear power stations which produce 79% of all energy; the USA has over 100 commercial nuclear power stations and in 2006, 20% of its energy came from nuclear power stations*

p 11, activity 3b

Befürworter: Was halten Sie von Atomenergie? Ich persönlich finde sie sehr wichtig und ich bin der Ansicht, dass sie langfristig dazu beiträgt, unseren Energiebedarf zu sichern. Andere europäische Länder glauben das auch. Ich denke da besonders an Frankreich, wo mehr als 50 Kernkraftwerke 79% der gesamten Energie produzieren. Auch in den USA kamen im Jahr 2006 20% der Energieproduktion des Landes

	aus Atomkraftwerken. Es gibt dort über 100 kommerzielle Kernkraftwerke.
Gegner:	Atomenergie soll ja sauber und effizient sein, aber meiner Meinung nach sollten wir lieber die erneuerbaren Energiequellen weiterentwickeln. Sie sind zwar momentan noch teuer, aber es gibt noch ein unheimlich großes Wachstumspotential in Deutschland – zum Beispiel in der Solarenergie und der Geothermie. Alternative Energiequellen sind nicht nur nachhaltig, sondern auch viel sicherer. Denken Sie nur an das Risiko eines Reaktorunfalls. Selbst bei neueren Kernkraftwerken gibt es keine totale Sicherheit.
Befürworter:	Aber denken Sie doch an die Arbeitsplätze, die die Atomkraftwerke schaffen. In Sellafield in Cumbria zum Beispiel verdienen ungefähr 6000 Angestellte ihren Lebensunterhalt durch Arbeit im Atomkraftwerk. Keiner von ihnen will natürlich seine Arbeit verlieren.
Gegner:	Da haben Sie Recht, aber vergessen Sie nicht, dass die Entwicklung der alternativen Energiequellen auch Arbeitsplätze schafft. Und ein weiteres Risiko der Atomkraft ist, dass man bis heute nicht genau weiß, wie groß das Gesundheitsrisiko ist. Es ist durchaus möglich, dass sich das Krebsrisiko, vor allem Leukämie, bei Leuten, die in der Nähe eines Kernkraftwerks wohnen, erhöht. Davor warnen auch manche Umweltorganisationen.
Befürworter:	Wie Sie wissen, ist das aber noch nicht bewiesen …
Gegner:	Genau und deshalb sollte man nichts riskieren. Sie dürfen meiner Meinung nach nicht den größten Unsicherheitsfaktor vergessen und das ist die Entsorgung des Atommülls. Haben Sie darauf eine Antwort?

3c Students complete the sentences with the most appropriate word.

Answers:

a *den größten Teil*
b *verlieren*
c *weniger als ein Viertel*
d *sicherer*
e *giftigem Material*

4 Students read the text on page 10 and their notes from activity 3b again. In preparation for activity 5, they then think of further arguments for and against nuclear power to add to each list.

5 Split the class in to two groups, 'for nuclear power' and 'against nuclear power'. The groups have a discussion on this topic.

6 Students write a letter to a newspaper or a blog either on the danger of nuclear energy or on nuclear energy being safer in the future. They should aim to write about 150 words. Encourage them to draw upon the ideas and vocabulary they have met on these pages.

Prüfungstraining

Grammar and skills

- Revise the tenses
- Complete gap-fill activities

Materials

- Students' Book pages 12–13
- CD 1, track 5
- *Arbeitsblätter* 4,5

1 Students complete the sentences with a verb in the correct form of the perfect tense.

Answers:

a *Im letzten Jahr* ***hat*** *das Bundesumweltministerium im Bereich der erneuerbaren Energien mehr als 150 Forschungsprojekte* ***bewilligt****.*
b *Zur selben Zeit* ***hat*** *man bereits 100 Projekte* ***abgeschlossen****.*
c *Diese Projekte* ***haben*** *viele neue Arbeitsplätze* ***geschaffen****.*
d *Der Umweltminister* ***ist*** *zur Eröffnung eines Projekts nach München* ***gefahren****.*
e *Die meisten Schüler* ***haben*** *den Jahresbericht zur Forschungsförderung beim Bundesumweltministerium kostenlos* ***bestellt****.*

2 Students write the sentences in the imperfect tense.

Answers:

a *Der Bundesumweltminister* ***eröffnete*** *eine internationale Konferenz zur Endlagerung radioaktiver Abfälle.*
b *Die Konferenz* ***sollte*** *einen Überblick über die neuesten Ergebnisse der verschiedenen nationalen Endlagerprogramme vermitteln.*
c *Bei der Konferenz* ***ging*** *es um technische und gesellschaftliche Herausforderungen bei der Standortfindung.*

d *Der Bundesumweltminister* ***lehnte*** *den Standort Gorleben als Atommüllendlager* ***ab****.*

e *Die Politiker und die Bürger* ***machten*** *sich Sorgen um die Endlagerung radioaktiver Abfälle.*

3 Students write the text in the pluperfect tense.

Answers:

Das Technische Hilfswerk ***hatte*** *sehr oft nach Naturkatastrophen und schweren Erdbeben* ***geholfen****, besonders bei der Wasserversorgung. Nach Erdbeben oder schweren Stürmen* ***war*** *die Wasserversorgung für die Bevölkerung total* ***zusammengebrochen****. Die Experten des Technischen Hilfswerks* ***waren*** *darauf spezialisiert* ***gewesen****, die Wasseraufbereitung so schnell wie möglich wieder zu sichern. Die Firma Kärcher* ***hatte*** *eine mobile Wasseraufbereitungsanlage zur Verfügung* ***gestellt****, um Menschen in Krisengebieten mit Trinkwasser zu versorgen.*

4 Students study the picture and then write a short paragraph entitled *Wie wird unsere Umwelt in 30 Jahren aussehen?* about how the environment will be in thirty years time. Remind them to use the future tense.

5 Students listen to the report and then fill in the missing numbers in the passage. Before attempting this activity, read the *Tipp* on page 7 again as a class.

Answers:

3,8 *Prozent der Arbeitnehmer in ganz Deutschland waren im Jahr 2002 im Umweltschutz beschäftigt. Das heißt, dass in dieser Branche* ***1,5*** *Millionen arbeiteten. Im Jahr* ***1998*** *bot der Bereich der alternativen Energiequellen* ***66 000*** *Menschen einen Arbeitsplatz. Im Jahr* ***2002*** *waren es über* ***118 000****. Innerhalb von nur* ***4*** *Jahren gab es rund* ***80*** *Prozent mehr Jobs. Allein im Bereich Windenergie fanden* ***38 000*** *Menschen eine Stelle. Damit lag dieser Bereich an der Spitze. Auch bei der Ausfuhr von umweltfreundlichen Waren gab es einen Anstieg von* ***25 000*** *Arbeitsplätzen.*

p 13, activity 5

Nach einer Studie des Deutschen Instituts für Wirtschaftsforschung steigen die Beschäftigungszahlen im Bereich Umweltschutz. Im Jahr 2002 waren rund 1,5 Millionen Menschen im Umweltschutz beschäftigt. Das sind 3,8 Prozent aller Angestellten und mehr als in der Autoindustrie oder im Maschinenbau. Dabei handelt es sich um eine Vielzahl verschiedener Berufe, von Biolandwirten und Recyclingmitarbeitern bis zu Umweltmanagern.

Der Umweltschutz ist also ein wichtiger Arbeitsfaktor auf dem deutschen Arbeitsmarkt. Besonders im Bereich der erneuerbaren Energien wird ein Anstieg an Arbeitsplätzen deutlich. Während im Jahr 1998 66 000 Leute beschäftigt waren, gab es 2002 ungefähr 118 700, was einen Anstieg von fast 80 Prozent bedeutet, und dies nur innerhalb von vier Jahren. Die Windkraft lag an der Spitze mit 38 000 Arbeitsplätzen.

Der Export von Umweltschutzprodukten hat ebenfalls neue Arbeitsplätze geschaffen, und zwar 25 000 mehr als im Jahr 1998, und durch Investitionen in den Umweltschutz gab es im Jahr 2002 35 000 mehr Stellen als 1998. In den Bereichen Klimaschutz, Ökodienstleistungen und Gebäudewirtschaft sowie durch Energieeinsparung soll es auch zukünftig steigende Beschäftigungschancen geben.

[Vera Gaserow, "Umweltschutz schafft neue Jobs", in: Frankfurter Rundschau vom 16. April 2004 in Informationen zur politischen Bildung Nr. 28/ 2005, p.34]

A 5

6 Students read the text and complete the sentences on the copymaster with the words that make the most sense.

Zur Auswahl

Skills focus

- Revision of the unit

Materials

- Students' Book page 14
- Solo CD, track 2

1 Students work in pairs and read the text in the speech bubbles. Each partner chooses one of the texts and prepares a list of arguments and examples to try and persuade the other to change his/her point of view.

2 Students listen to the report about wind farms and answer the questions to test comprehension.

Answers:

a *vor einem Jahr*

b *die Windräder verschandeln die Landschaft. Auch stört der Lärm.*

c *Im ersten Jahr haben sie zehnmal so viel Strom erzeugt, wie die 3000 Haushalte in Westerau in einem Jahr verbrauchen.*

d *Rundherum werden weitere Windkraftanlagen geplant.*
e *Mehrere Anwohner haben Widerspruch gegen diese Pläne eingelegt.*
f *Er hat gerade seine Wohnung mit 20% Verlust verkauft, weil niemand gern einen Blick auf Windräter hat.*

p 14, activity 2

Westerau: Für die Einwohner dieser kleinen Gemeinde hat eine neue Methode der Energiegewinnung die Lebensqualität drastisch vermindert. Sechs 70 Meter hohe Windanlagen wurden vor einem Jahr am Rande des Dorfes gebaut. Seitdem beklagen sich manche Einwohner darüber, dass die Windräter die Landschaft verschandeln. Auch stört der Lärm. Das Zischen der Räder sei, meinte eine Dorfbewohnerin, ständig zu hören. Vom Standpunkt der Energiegewinnung aus, sind die Räder ein Erfolg gewesen. Im ersten Jahr haben sie zehnmal so viel Strom erzeugt, wie die 3000 Haushalte in Westerau in einem Jahr verbrauchen. Rundherum werden weitere Windkraftanlagen geplant. Mehrere Anwohner haben jedoch Widerspruch gegen diese Pläne eingelegt. Besonders betroffen ist Kaufmann Holger Veith, dessen Haus in direkter Nähe der Anlagen steht. Er hat keine Lust, weitere Anlagen direkt vor den Augen zu haben. Auch finanzielle Folgen erschweren das Leben der Westerauer – Udo Wiche hat gerade seine Wohnung mit 20% Verlust verkauft, weil niemand gern einen Blick auf Windräder hat.

3a Students read the text, *Windkraft in Deutschland*. They then look up the words in a dictionary and find synonyms for them in the reading text.

Answers:

a *Energie gewinnen – to produce/tap energy – Energie liefern*
b *Standorte – site – Niederlassungen*
c *unterscheiden – to distinguish – auszeichnen*
d *markant – prominent – führend*
e *entwickeln – to open up – erschließen*
f *nicht ausreichend – in short supply – knapp*

3b Students decide which of the sentences are true (R), false (F) or not in the text (N).

Answers:

a R **b** N **c** F **d** F **e** R **f** N **g** R

Umweltschutz Einheit 2

Unit objectives

By the end of this unit students will be able to:

- Discuss pros and cons of recycling
- Explain and discuss the role of pressure groups
- Discuss the issues of a sustainable lifestyle
- Discuss the consequences of climate change for developing countries
- Discuss the responsibility of the industrial countries

Grammar

By the end of this unit students will be able to:

- Use modal verbs with the passive

Skills

By the end of this unit students will be able to:

- Translate from German into English

Materials

- Students' Book page 15

1 Students read the captions on the topic of pollution and place them in them in order of importance based on their own opinion. They then explain why they have ranked them as they have and compare and discuss it with the rest of the class.

Recycling

Grammar focus

- Revise the passive

Materials

- Students' Book pages 16–17
- CD 1, track 6
- Grammar Workbook page 64

1 Students work in groups to discuss what they think of recycling and what they recycle at home.

2a Students read the two opposing views.

2b Students decide which point of view they agree with. They then put forward arguments for their viewpoint, first with a partner and then in a class debate.

3a Students match the German expressions with the appropriate English translation.

Answers:

a 5 **b** 3 **c** 4 **d** 7 **e** 8 **f** 2 **g** 1 **h** 6

3b Students listen to two short reports about unusual ways of recycling.

p 16, activities 3b and 3c

Recycelte Produkte – wer kauft die schon? OK, durch die Wiederverwertung werden zwar Kohlendioxyd, Wasser, Bleichmittel und andere Stoffe eingespart, man tut also was für unseren Planeten, aber jetzt mal im Ernst!

Wenn Sie bis jetzt auch so gedacht haben, sollten Sie einmal die edlen Boutiquen in Bremen und in anderen deutschen Großstädten besuchen. Dort werden nämlich todschicke Recycling-Taschen verkauft. Die originellen Taschen werden aus alten Autoreifenteilen und nicht mehr benutzten südafrikanischen Nummernschildern hergestellt.

Sie fragen sich nun sicher: warum südafrikanische Nummernschilder? In Südafrika werden nämlich die Taschen entworfen und produziert und dann nach Bremen exportiert, wo jede Tasche als Designertasche in teuren Boutiquen und Fachgeschäften verkauft wird.

Beim nächsten Projekt geht es um Altpapierrecycling. Na und? Was soll daran schon originell sein? Das gibt es doch schon lange.

Richtig, aber wenn man aus altem benutzten Papier wieder Neues herstellen will, wird dabei eine Menge Wasser und Energie verbraucht. Die Direkt Recycelte Papierprodukte GmbH recycelt Papier ohne Umwege, wobei alles neu zugeschnitten, gefaltet und geklebt wird. Die Firma stellt Briefumschläge und Büromaterial her. Dabei spart man sowohl 100 Prozent Wasser als auch Binde- und Bleichmittel. Zwischen 5 und 10 Prozent des gesamten Altpapiers in Deutschland – das sind rund 4,5 Millionen Tonnen – lassen sich auf diese Weise wiederverwerten.

3c To test comprehension, students read the phrases and decide whether they are true (R) or false (F). There are five false statements. They correct the false statements.

Answers:

a *R*
b *R*

c *F – Recycelte Taschen gibt es auch in anderen deutschen Großstädten zu kaufen.*
d *F – Die Taschen werden in Südafrika hergestellt.*
e *R*
f *F – Diese Taschen werden in edlen Boutiquen angeboten.*
g *R*
h *F – Die Firma stellt Briefumschläge und Büromaterial her.*
i *F – Bei der neuen Methode werden keine Binde- und Bleichmittel benutzt.*
j *R*

4 Students read the statement and write a paragraph saying if they agree with it. They should justify their point of view.

5a Students read the text, *Was geschieht eigentlich mit unserem Altglas?.*

5b Students answer the questions on the reading text.

Answers:
a *Er sollte die Flaschen ausspülen und in einen Glascontainer werfen.*
b *Es gibt grüne, weiße und braune Flaschen.*
c *Das Altglas wird mehrmals farbsortiert und zerkleinert, bis daraus ein Granulat wird.*
d *in einer Glashütte*
e *Der Rohstoff wird in Formmaschinen gefüllt, wo er zu Flaschen geformt wird.*
f *mehr als 50 Milliarden*

Grammatik

A Students read the text about *Altglas* again, write out all the passive forms and translate them into English.

B Students put the sentences into the passive.

Answers:
a *Altglas wird gesäubert und sortiert.*
b *Taschen aus alten Autoteilen wurden in vielen Boutiquen verkauft.*
c *Meinem Bruder ist gezeigt worden, wie er den Müll trennen sollte.*

Umweltschutz und Nachhaltigkeit

Skills focus

- Translating from German into English

Materials

- Students' Book pages 18–19
- CD 1, track 7
- *Arbeitsblätter* 6, 7

1 Students study each of the newspaper extracts. They then work with a partner and discuss what they think of the action taken in each of the extracts and whether they would take part in a strike or demonstration.

2a Students read the newspaper report about a Greenpeace protest in Vienna.

2b Students match the phrases.

Answers:
a 5 **b** 3 **c** 4 **d** 1 **e** 2

2c Students complete the sentences with the most appropriate ending.

Answers:
a 2 **b** 3 **c** 2 **d** 3 **e** 1

3 Students translate the first section of the text on page 18 into English. Refer them to the *Tipp* before attempting this.

4a Students listen to the interview with two members of BUND and note down which projects are mentioned.

Answer:
BUND want the Federal Government to raise taxes on cars with a high carbon dioxide output and to reduce taxes on cars with a low carbon dioxide output. They also think that cars with a CO_2 output of under 100g/km shouldn't be taxed.
They also want to retain animal and plant species, and to retain meadows and preserve them as habitats for flora and fauna.

p 19, activities 4a and 4b

Interviewer: Guten Tag, Frau Probst und Herr Berger, und willkommen bei uns im Studio. Sie sind beide aktive Mitglieder bei der Organisation BUND, und ich würde Ihnen gern einige Fragen zu Ihrer Arbeit stellen. Erklären Sie uns als Erstes doch bitte, wofür der der Name „BUND" steht.

Frau Probst: Es steht für Bund für Umwelt und Naturschutz in Deutschland.

Interviewer: Danke. Frau Probst, mit welchen Aktionen oder Themen beschäftigt sich BUND zur Zeit?

Frau Probst:	Es gibt da eine ganze Menge. Für mich ist es besonders wichtig, dass die Bundesregierung endlich die Steuer für Autos mit einem hohen Kohlendioxidausstoß erhöht, aber für Autos mit geringerem CO_2-Ausstoß senkt. Bis jetzt blockiert der Bundeswirtschaftsminister diese Kfz-Steuer-Reform. Wir bei BUND aber fordern, dass neue Autos, deren Kohlendioxid-Ausstoß unter 100 Gramm CO_2 pro Kilometer liegt, ganz von der Kfz-Steuer befreit werden.
Interviewer:	Und wie ist das bei Ihnen, Herr Berger?
Herr Berger:	Ich mache mir Sorgen um genmanipulierte Nahrungsmittel und Nanopartikel in unseren Lebensmitteln. Diese unsichtbaren Nanopartikel sind in Verpackungen, Lebensmitteln und Küchenartikeln enthalten.
Interviewer:	Warum genau sind Sie gegen diese Nanopartikel?
Herr Berger:	Nun, bis jetzt weiß man noch nicht, welche Gefahren und Risiken diese Nanomaterialien langfristig mit sich bringen. Es gibt zwar immer mehr wissenschaftliche Beweise für mögliche Gesundheits- und Umweltrisiken, doch man braucht einfach noch mehr Studien, um diese Partikel auf mögliche Risiken zu prüfen. Bis man zu einem eindeutigen Ergebnis kommt, sollte man Produkte, die diese Nanomaterialien enthalten, nicht verkaufen.
Frau Probst:	In einem weiteren wichtigen Projekt für mich geht es darum, die biologische Vielfalt an Tier- und Pflanzenarten zu erhalten.
Interviewer:	Ist das denn wirklich so ein großes Problem?
Frau Probst:	Auf jeden Fall, denn Deutschland hat im Vergleich zu anderen europäischen Ländern sehr kleine Naturschutzgebiete. Besonders die Buchen sind in den Wäldern gefährdet. In Deutschland gibt es auch nur noch wenige Streuobstwiesen, und BUND will diese erhalten, denn bis zu 5000 Tierarten haben dort ihr Habitat. In keinem anderen europäischen Land gibt es mehr bedrohte Pflanzen- und Tierarten als hier bei uns in der Bundesrepublik.
Interviewer:	Ich bedanke mich bei Ihnen für dieses informative Gespräch und wünsche Ihnen viel Erfolg bei Ihren Aktionen.

4b Students decide which of the statements are true (R), which are false (F) and which are not in the text (N), to check understanding.

Answers:
a F **b** R **c** R **d** N **e** R **f** F **g** F

5 Students work with a partner and discuss which of the projects mentioned in the listening passage they would support and why. They then discuss this as a class.

6 Students write a summary on the topic of working for an environmental organisation. How effective are they and would they support them? They should give reasons for their opinions. Encourage them to use the ideas and vocabulary presented on these pages of the Students' Book.

Globale Verantwortung

Materials

- Students' Book pages 20–21
- CD 1, tracks 8–9
- *Arbeitsblatt* 8

1 Students study the pictures. As a class, they then discuss how we can put these principles into practice in today's society.

2a Students read the text.

2b Students read the text again and find the German for the words or phrases listed.

Answers:
a *gedankenlos*
b *Wüsten*
c *spüren*
d *Dürren*
e *Ausbeutung*
f *auf Kosten*
g *Lebensgrundlagen*
h *erkennen*

2c A reading comprehension activity. Students read the text again and answer the questions.

Answers:
a *Sie fördern einen gedankenlosen Ressourcenverbrauch, der viele Umweltprobleme verursacht.*
b *Die negative Auswirkungen sind nicht nur im reichen Westen, sondern auf der ganzen Welt zu spüren.*
c *Wenn wir im reichen Westen unseren bisherigen Lebensstil beibehalten, geht das nur auf Kosten der armen Länder und wir gefährden ihre Lebensgrundlagen.*

d *Die Umweltbelastung für die ganze Welt würde sich vervielfachen mit dramatischen Folgen.*
e Student's own answer
f Student's own answer

2d Students work with a partner to study the main arguments presented in the reading text. They then try to find counter arguments for these. Finally, they compare these with the rest of the class.

3a Students listen to the recording.

p 21, activities 3a and 3b

Zur Zeit produziert jeder Erdbewohner durchschnittlich ungefähr 4 Tonnen CO_2 pro Jahr. Nach Berechnungen von Klimaforschern ist es notwendig, die CO_2-Emissionen um 50% zu reduzieren, wenn wir den Klimawandel stoppen wollen. Ein realistisches, nachhaltiges Niveau wäre etwa 1,7 Tonnen CO_2 pro Jahr. In den westlichen Industrieländern sind wir jedoch weit von diesem Ziel entfernt, wenn man bedenkt, dass ein europäischer Durchschnittsbürger 8 Tonnen, ein amerikanischer Durchschnittsbürger sogar fast 20 Tonnen CO_2 produziert. Vergleicht man diese Zahlen mit denen der Entwicklungsländer, so sieht man, dass die CO_2-Emissionen pro Kopf dort unter dem nachhaltigen Niveau liegen, also unter 1,7 Tonnen. Die Entwicklungsländer könnten also ihren Pro-Kopf-Verbrauch und damit den Lebensstandard ihrer Bevölkerung erhöhen, wenn wir unsere Pro-Kopf-Emissionen drastisch reduzieren würden. Diese Beispiele zeigen deutlich, bei wem die globale Verantwortung letztendlich liegt. Dennoch ist es kaum zu erwarten, dass sich unsere politischen und wirtschaftlichen Institutionen grundlegend und langfristig ändern werden.

3b Students complete the sentences by filling in the appropriate figures.

Answers:
a 50 **b** 1,7 **c** 8; 6,3 **d** 18,3

4a Students listen to the recording about the development of international environmental policies.

p 21, activities 4a and 4b

Umweltprobleme wie Klimawandel oder giftige Abfälle in den Meeren betreffen nicht nur einzelne Staaten, sondern sind länderübergreifend. Auch die wirtschaftlichen Entwicklungen und die Globalisierung hatten mehr internationale Zusammenarbeit zur Folge. So kam es 1972 in Stockholm zur ersten internationalen Konferenz der Vereinten Nationen, bei der Industrie- und Entwicklungsländer gemeinsam zu Umweltproblemen Stellung nahmen.

Zu dieser Zeit gab es jedoch bereits verschiedene regionale Umweltabkommen wie das Abkommen zum Schutz der Nordsee im Jahr 1972. Im Jahr 1979 fand das Genfer Übereinkommen statt, in dem die Bekämpfung der Luftverschmutzung in Europa durch ‚sauren Regen' diskutiert wurde. Bis 2005 wurden eine ganze Menge verschiedener regionaler Umweltabkommen getroffen. Im Jahr 1991 wurde die „Globale Umweltfazilität" gegründet, um globale Umweltprobleme in armen Ländern zu finanzieren. Mit der wachsenden Globalisierung seit der zweiten Hälfte der 80er Jahre wird die Umweltpolitik zunehmend als internationales Thema betrachtet.

4b To check comprehension, students state which of the sentences are true (R) and which are false (F). They correct any false sentences.

Answers:
a *F – im Jahr 1972*
b *F – der Nordsee*
c *R*
d *R*
e *F – in armen Ländern*

5 Students work with a partner and discuss what they think of the claim that rich, industrialised countries should fundamentally change their lifestyle. They also consider how these countries should do this. Finally they discuss this as a class. Encourage them to use the ideas and vocabulary presented on these pages of the Students' Book in their discussion.

6 Students write an essay of approximately 150–200 words, giving their own opinion on the questions raised in activity 5.

Prüfungstraining

Grammar and skills

- The passive
- Translating from German into English

Materials

- Students' Book pages 22–23
- Grammar Workbook page 64
- *Arbeitsblatt* 9

Grammatik

A Students decide which of the sentences listed are in the passive and what tense they are.

Answers:
b – present; d – imperfect; e – perfect; f – imperfect

B Students translate the sentences into German.

Answers:
- **a** *Heutzutage kann fast alles wiederverwertet werden.*
- **b** *Die leeren Flaschen mussten von meinem Bruder zur Sammelstelle gebracht werden.*
- **c** *Gefährdete Tierarten sollten geschützt werden.*
- **d** *Mehr Naturschutzgebiete sollten errichtet werden.*
- **e** *Die tropischen Regenwälder dürfen nicht abgeholzt werden.*
- **f** *Unsere Situation kann verbessert werden, wenn alle zum Umweltschutz beitragen.*

1 Students read the text and complete the sentences using the correct form of the verbs in brackets.

Answers:
*Sind moderne Geräte wirklich sparsamer im Energieverbrauch als die alten? Diese Frage **wird** oft von Verbrauchern **gestellt**. Nun **soll** durch die ‚Öko-Design-Richtlinie' dafür **gesorgt werden**, dass es tatsächlich so sein wird. So **wird** für Fernseher, Waschmaschinen und andere elektrische Geräte **festgelegt**, wie viel Energie **verbraucht werden darf**, wenn sie in Betrieb sind und wenn sie im Standby-Modus sind. Diese Information **soll** den Kunden zur Verfügung **gestellt werden**, wenn sie ein neues Gerät kaufen wollen. Es **muss** auch **erwähnt werden**, wie viel Strom man sparen kann, wenn der Fernseher zum Beispiel ganz **ausgeschaltet** und nicht im Standby **gelassen wird**.*

2 Students put the active sentences into the passive, making sure that they use the correct tense.

Answers:
- **a** *Das Genfer Übereinkommen zur Bekämpfung der grenzüberschreitenden Luftverschmutzung in Europa ist im Jahr 1979 unterzeichnet worden.*
- **b** *1991 wurde die Globale Umweltfazilität gegründet.*
- **c** *Auf den Umweltkonferenzen wird von den teilnehmenden Ländern über globale Umweltprobleme diskutiert.*
- **d** *Es muss entschieden werden, welche Länder besonders für die Luftverschmutzung verantwortlich sind.*
- **e** *Heutzutage werden bereits Grundschüler über Umweltprobleme informiert.*

3a Students read the text.

3b Students look at the list of nouns from the text and discuss with a partner what they might mean.

3c Students read the text again and write out all verbs in the passive. They then check what tense the passive forms are in and if the subject is singular or plural. Finally, they translate them into English.

Answers:
…werden Vorschläge für die Verwertung von Altmetall und Elektroschrott sowie Altpapier und Bauschuttrecycling vorgestellt. – *…suggestions for exploiting scrap metal and electrical junk as well as how to recycle waste paper and building rubble are put forward.*

…sollen so wenig Ressourcen wie möglich verbraucht werden oder zumindest sollen sie so effizient wie möglich eingesetzt werden. – *…as few resources as possible should be used or at least they should be used as efficiently as possible.*

In Ruanda wurde mit dem ruandischen Umweltminister ein Plan für die Abfallwirtschaft des Landes erarbeitet… – *In Rwanda, a plan for the country's refuse industry was worked out with the Rwandan minister for the environment…*

3d Students choose the translation which fits best for each of the phrases.

Answers:
- **a** *waste disposal*
- **b** *ambitious plans*
- **c** *superfluous*
- **d** *shall be used*
- **e** *refuse industry*

3e Students read the first sentence again and look up the conjunctions *denn* and *wie* in a dictionary. They should read all definitions given and find the most suitable translation for this first sentence.

3f Students translate the whole text. They then compare their work with others in the class to find the best possible translation.

Zur Auswahl

Skills focus
- Translating from German into English

Materials
- Students' Book page 24
- Solo CD, track 3
- *Arbeitsblatt* 10

1a Students read the text.

1b Students fill in the gaps with the correct form of the words in the box. There are more words than spaces!

Answers:

a *verbringt*
b *erneuert werden; Modelle*
c *werden; freigesetz*
d *verschwendet*
e *Lärmbelastung; Stress*

1c Students present a proposal to the class on how they would make the office more ecologically sound. They should look at the *Naturschutzbunds Deutschland* website (www.nabu.de) for ideas.

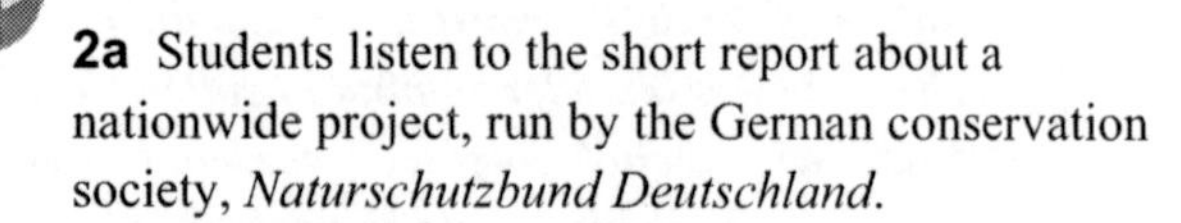

2a Students listen to the short report about a nationwide project, run by the German conservation society, *Naturschutzbund Deutschland.*

p 24, activities 2a and 2b

Im Jahr 2006 gingen in der Bundesrepublik pro Tag 106 Hektar Landesfläche durch den Bau von neuen Siedlungen und den Ausbau des Verkehrsnetzes verloren. Wenn das so weiter geht, wird es verheerende Folgen für Menschen, Tiere und Pflanzen haben, da ihr Lebensraum dadurch beeinträchtigt und irreversibel geschädigt wird. Obwohl die Bundesregierung in der nationalen Nachhaltigkeitsstrategie den Flächenverbrauch bis zum Jahr 2020 auf 30 Hektar pro Tag reduzieren will, hat sich bis jetzt noch nicht viel geändert, und der Flächenverbrauch ist fast noch gleich hoch. Wenn aber immer mehr Naturlandschaften durch Siedlungen oder neue Straßen ‚zerschnitten' werden, werden die naturnahen Lebensräume zu Inseln, und der Lebensraum für Tiere und Pflanzen wird immer knapper. NABU, der Naturschutzbund Deutschland, will nun mit Kommunen zusammenarbeiten, um eine nachhaltige Siedlungsentwicklung zu gewährleisten. Das Projekt soll im Jahr 2009 starten und zunächst drei Jahre dauern.

[from: www.nabu.de 'Partner für die Natur gesucht']

2b To check they have understood the recording, students read the statements and decide whether each one is true (R), false (F), or not mentioned in the text (N). They then correct any false statements.

Answers:

a *F – 2006 wurde die Landesfläche täglich um 106 Hektar reduziert.*
b *R*
c *F – Die Folgen für die Menschen sind genauso schlimm wie für die Tiere und Pflanzen.*
d *N*
e *F – der Lebensraum wird knapper und umgeben von Siedlungen wie eine Insel*
f *R*
g *F – Das Projekt soll im Jahr 2009 beginnen.*

3 Students translate the sentences into English. Encourage them to read the *Tipp* on page 19 of the Students' Book first.

Possible answers:

a *Each year in the federal republic, more than 100 hectares of land is lost per day through the construction of new housing estates and improving the transport system.*
b *The German conservation society, Naturschutzbund Deutschland, offers community the opportunity to work together with them on this project.*
c *The incessant noise of the air conditioning can have a negative effect on the health of office workers.*

4 Students read the list of different environmental problems and rank them in what they consider the order of importance. They should then say why they have ordered them as they have.

Wiederholung Einheit 1–2

Materials

- Students' Book pages 25–26
- CD 1, track 10

1a Students read the text about the development of solar energy.

1b Students read the statements and choose the best phrase to complete them.

Answers:

a 3 **b** 1 **c** 2 **d** 1 **e** 2 **f** 2

2 Students answer the questions orally.

3a Students listen to the report about cars in the future and then list the words a–g in the order in which they hear them.

Answers:

c, b, e, d, a, f, g

p 25, activities 3a and 3b

Schon vor fünfzig Jahren experimentierte man mit der Holzvergasertechnologie, doch ist man in der Zwischenzeit mit Alternativen nur langsam vorangekommen.

Erst die große Krise von 1973 hat wieder daran erinnert, dass die Abhängigkeit vom Mineralöl uns letzen Endes mehr schadet als nützt und dass die fossilen Energiequellen doch irgendwie bald erschöpft sein werden. Und trotz aller Bemühungen verbrauchen die Autos heute noch mehr Benzin als damals, teilweise wegen des größeren Verkehrsaufkommens, andererseits aber auch, weil der Verbraucher nicht auf große, rasante und Benzin schluckende Wagen verzichten will.

Seitdem haben Firmen mit mehr oder weniger großem Erfolg an der Herstellung von Ökobenzin gearbeitet. In Sachsen erforscht eine keine High-Tech-Firma die Umwandlung von Biomasse in Brennstoff. Biomasse besteht aus Holz- oder Pflanzenresten und somit wäre die Spritproduktion ziemlich umweltfreundlich, obwohl wiederum Kohlendioxid entsteht. Der Wasserstoff wird von den Pflanzen wieder aufgenommen und somit ist der Wiederverwertungskreis komplett.
Im Moment sind diese Versuche nur ein Experiment. In fünf Jahren jedoch soll die Großproduktion laufen. Der Liter Ökobenzin soll 65 Cent kosten und wird von der Regierung subventioniert werden.

Gleichzeitig wird an Elektromotoren, Leichtbauwerkstoffen, Batterien und weiteren alternativen Brennstoff gearbeitet.

Bundesumweltminister Jürgen Trittin meinte, die Regierung Kohl habe in dieser Richtung einiges versäumt, was die neue rot-grüne Koalition nachholen werde. Immerhin werden in den nächtsten paar Jahren 153 Millionen Euro zur Erforschung alternativer Energien ausgegeben und außerdem sei es ein für alle Mal klargestellt, dass die Mineralölkonzerne und die fossile Energiewirtschaft nicht das letzte Wort haben werden.

3b Students listen to the report again and choose which word best fills each gap.

Answers:
a 1 **b** 2 **c** 2 **d** 1 **e** 3 **f** 3 **g** 3

4 Students translate the passage into English.

Answer:
Not only numerous unsolved problems, but also many open questions await participants of the 2008 UN conservation conference in Bonn. Themes range from concern over the growth of the world population, which of course brings with it big nutritional problems, to a sustainable, global energy supply.

Due to the boom of using raw materials that can be grown again as sources of energy, as in Brazil, for example, where sugar cane is cultivated for the production of organic petrol, pressure is growing to further clear exisiting nature reserves. Through this, however, the biodiversity in these areas can be endangered.

5a Students draw upon the ideas and vocabulary they have met on these pages to discuss which they consider to be more important, using sugar cane plantations for organic petrol or the preservation of the tropical rainforest. They should give reasons for their views.

5b Students use the notes from the discussion in activity 5a to produce an essay of 150–200 words.

Ausländer Einheit 3

Unit objectives

By the end of this unit students will be able to:

- Talk about the different groups of immigrants in Germany and their problems
- Discuss the problems of second- and third-generation immigrants
- Discuss the reasons for racism and its effects
- Discuss the integration of foreigners

Grammar

By the end of this unit students will be able to:

- Use the subjunctive

Skills

By the end of this unit students will be able to:

- Translate into German

Materials

- Students' Book page 27

1 As a class, students study the pictures and then discuss questions a–d.

Wer sind die Ausländer?

Key language

- *Es gibt vier Gruppen von Ausländern in Deutschland.*
- *... kommen aus ...*
- *Die ... sind nach Deutschland gekommen, weil ...*
- *Sie haben das Recht ...*
- *Sie dürfen/dürfen nicht ...*

Materials

- Students' Book pages 28–29
- CD 1, track 11
- *Arbeitsblatt* 11

1 As a class, dicuss the questions about immigrants: Are there many immigrants in your area? Where are they from? Why did they emigrate?

2a Students read the texts.

2b Students match each word with its definition.

Answers:

a 2 **b** 5 **c** 7 **d** 1 **e** 6 **f** 8 **g** 4 **h** 3

2c Students match the sentence halves.

Answers:

a 6 **b** 1 **c** 10 **d** 2 **e** 7 **f** 11 **g** 3 **h** 5 **i** 9 **j** 4 **k** 8

3 Students listen and note down the statistics for a–j.

Answers:

a *7,3 Mio.*
b *1,5 Mio.*
c *29%*
d *6%*
e *42%*
f *3,2 Mio.*
g *200 000*
h *468 000*
i *34 000*
j *4.4%*

p 29, activity 3

Interviewer: Frau Nolde, können Sie uns etwas über Ausländer in Deutschland erzählen?

Brigitte Nolde: Ungefähr 7,3 Millionen Ausländer wohnen in Deutschland. Rund 1,5 Millionen sind in Deutschland geboren, haben aber die Staatsbürgerschaft der Eltern. Diese Ausländer sind hauptsächlich die Kinder der Gastarbeiter, die in den 60er Jahren zu uns gekommen sind. Diese Gastarbeiter haben ein niedrigeres Einkommen als die meisten Deutschen und auch geringere Qualifikationen. 29% der Gastarbeiter haben keinen Schulabschluss. Bei der zweiten Generation ist die Statistik deutlich besser. 42% der zweiten Generation sind höhere Angestellte, im Vergleich zu 6% der ersten Generation.
Die zweite Gruppe von Ausländern sind die Aussiedler. Die Aussiedler sind eigentlich keine Ausländer, sie gehören zu den 3,2 Millionen Menschen deutscher Abstammung, die in Osteuropa wohnen. Letztes Jahr kamen 200 000 Aussiedler nach Deutschland zurück. 97% kommen aus Russland, Polen oder Rumänien.

Die dritte Gruppe sind die Asylbewerber. Zum Höhepunkt der Asylwelle zur Zeit des Kreigs in Jugoslawien kamen 468 000 Asylanten nach Deutschland. 2006 waren es nur noch 34 000. Die meisten haben jedoch kein Recht auf Asyl. In der Regel werden 4,4% der Asylanträge anerkannt.

Ausländer bei uns

Materials

- Students' Book pages 30–31
- CD 1, track 12
- *Arbeitsblätter* 12, 13, 14

1 Students read and categorise the sentences. They then discuss them in class.

Answers:

- a *Aussiedler*
- b *Asylanten*
- c *Asylanten*
- d *Asylanten*
- e *Wanderarbeiter*
- f *Wanderarbeiter*
- g *Asylanten*
- h *Aussiedler*
- i *Aussiedler*
- j *Asylanten*

2a Students read the texts about Fatima, Guljan and Marek.

2b Students complete the sentences using the words given. Point out that they will not need all of the words listed in the Students' book.

Answers:

- a *Fatimas Familie musste aus dem Iran **fliehen**.*
- b *Bis der Asylantrag **anerkannt** wurde, lebte die Familie in **Unsicherheit**.*
- c *Den Eltern fiel es schwerer als den Kindern, sich in Deutschland **einzuleben**.*
- d *Fatima hat leider **Ausländerfeindlichkeit** erlebt.*
- e *Guljans Vater hält Tradition und Kultur für sehr **wichtig**.*
- f *Im Vergleich zu ihren Freunden ist Guljans Freiheit sehr **beschränkt**.*
- g *Guljan hat es ihrer Familie **verheimlicht**, dass sie einen Freund hat.*
- h *Marek ist aus **persönlichen** Gründen nach Deutschland gezogen.*
- i *Die EU-Erweiterung hat es ihm **ermöglicht**, in Deutschland zu arbeiten.*
- j *Jan ist auch sehr **dankbar**, dass er einen besseren **Lohn** verdienen kann.*

2c Students answer the questions in German.

- a *Er wartete auf die Entscheidung über seinen Asylantrag.*
- b *Ihre Familie ist streng religiös und legt viel Wert auf ihre Kultur, aber sie hat auch viel Kontakt zu deutschen Mädchen und Jungen und hat jetzt einen Freund aus ihrer Klasse.*
- c *Er will in Polen ein Haus auf dem Land kaufen und arbeitet in Deutschland um sich das zu leisten.*

3a Students listen to Thomas' story and put the sentences in chronological order.

Answers:

b, c, d, e, a, f, g

p 31, activities 3 and 3b

Reporterin: Thomas wohnt mit seiner Familie in Bayern. Die Familie gehört zu den deutschen Aussiedlern aus der ehemaligen Sowjetunion.

Thomas: Meine Vorfahren zogen Mitte des neunzehnten Jahrhunderts in die Ukraine. Dort bekamen sie Land, gründeten eine Siedlung und bauten mit den anderen Siedlern zusammen Häuser, eine Schule und eine Kirche. Es war eine deutsche Siedlung, wie viele andere zu der Zeit. Meine Familie wohnte bis Ende des Zweiten Weltkriegs dort, dann begann Stalin die deutsche Minderheit zu verfolgen. Meine Großeltern wurden nach Kasachstan in Mittelasien deportiert. Dort wurden sie auch diskriminiert und als Faschisten beschimpft.

Reporterin: 1956 wurde Thomas' Vater Christian in Kasachstan geboren und seine Eltern haben sich in Moskau um die Ausreise in die alte Heimat beworben. Über 30 Jahre lang haben sie nichts gehört, dann in Jahr 1990 geschah ein Wunder – sie haben die Ausreiseerlaubnis bekommen. So konnten der 8-Jährige Thomas, seine Geschwister, Eltern und Großeltern in die Bundesrepublik reisen.

Thomas: Für meine Großeltern war es wie ein Traum. Sie hatten immer noch die alten Familienurkunden und konnten

	unsere Staatsangehörigkeit problemlos beweisen. Wir konnten aber keinen Besitz mitnehmen, meinen Eltern mussten ihr Haus verkaufen, um die Reise zu zahlen. Aber wir haben Begrübungsgeld von der Regierung bekommen. Die Familie wohnte ein paar Wochen in einem Lager, zog dann nach Bayern, wo ihre Vorfahren herkamen.
Reporterin:	Die Integration ging aber nicht so einfach. Thomas' Eltern hatten Schwierigkeiten, Arbeit zu finden, da sie im Vergleich zu den meisten Deutschen nur geringe Qualifikationen hatten. Auch die Sprache war ein Problem – ihr Deutsch war veraltet und vor allem seine Großeltern hatten Probleme mit der Umgangssprache.
Thomas:	Meine Großeltern haben die meisten Schwierigkeiten gehabt. Sie hatten ein Bild von Deutschland wie es vor fünfzig Jahren war, und hatten auch ein Idealbild von der Bundesrepublik. Das neue Deutschland ist ihnen sehr fremd. Die Vorurteile haben sie auch am härtesten getroffen – in Russland waren wir die Deutschen, hier werden wir von manchen als Russen angesehen, die nach Hause zurückkehren sollten.

3b Students match the sentence halves.

Answers:
a 4 **b** 1 **c** 7 **d** 8 **e** 2 **f** 3 **g** 5 **h** 6

4 Students write 250 words on the topic of why immigrants come to Germany and the problems they experience. Encourage them to use the vocabulary and ideas presented on these pages.

5 Students work in groups of four and have a group discussion. Each member of the group takes on one of the roles listed and they all interview one another. Before they begin, they should write down a list of questions to use during their interviews.

Rassismus

Materials

- Students' Book pages 32–33
- CD 1, track 13

1a Students read through the prejudices and decide which ones they think are the strongest.

1b Students now read the facts and match each fact to the corresponding prejudice.

Answers:
1 c **2** a **3** b **4** d **5** e **6** f

2a After students have read the text about the rise of the right-wing, they choose the appropriate heading for each paragraph of the text.

Answers:
a paragraph 3 **b** paragraph 5 **c** paragraph 1
d paragraph 4 **e** paragraph 2

2b Students now pick out the German words which match the definitions given.

Answers:
a *jagten*
b *eingeschränkt*
c *tabu*
d *notgedrungen*
e *ersetzen*
f *identifizierbar*

2c A true/false activity to test reading comprehension.

Answers:
a *F – Er hatte eine Stichwunde am Auge und ein gebrochenes Handgelenk.*
b *R*
c *N*
d *R*
e *R*
f *F – Sie ist nicht eingebettet in eine rechtsextreme Alltagskultur.*
g *N*
h *R*
i *F – Fast zwei Drittel der DVU-Wähler haben eine feste Tätigkeit.*
j *N*
k *F – Er zeigt Verständnis für Brandanschläge gegen Asylantenheime.*
l *R*

2d Students summarize the text in German in about 100 words.

3 Students listen to the interview with a member of a neo-Nazi group and answer questions a–h.

Answers:
a *durch seinen Bruder*
b *Sie nehmen die Jobs, oder sie leben vom Sozialgeld.*
c *Er glaubt, 15% der Bevölkerung seien Ausländer; es sind nur 1,8%.*

d *Er hat Ausländer aus den Kneipen und Nachtlokalen in der Stadt rausgeworfen. Keiner darf mehr rein.*
e *Weil sie was mit einem Türken hatte.*
f *Sie hat die Beziehung abgebrochen, weil es sonst für ihren Freund schlecht ausgesehen hätte.*
g *Er würde einen Angriff auf ein Asylantenheim machen.*
h *Probleme mit der Polizei, könnte seine Lehrstelle verlieren*

p 33, activity 3

Int: Heiko, Sie gehören einer rechtsextremen Gruppe an. Wie sind Sie zu dieser Clique gekommen?
Heiko: Mein Bruder war dabei und hat mich mitgenommen. Aber ich hatte ihn schon darum gebeten, weil ich derselben Meinung bin.
Int: Können Sie Ihre Meinung zum Thema Ausländer genau erklären?
Heiko: Deutschland gehört den Deutschen. Die anderen haben hier nichts zu suchen.
Int: Wie schaden Ihnen die Ausländer?
Heiko: Sie nehmen uns die Arbeit weg. Die Deutschen sitzen auf der Straße und sie haben Jobs. Oder sie leben auf unsere Kosten, vom Sozialgeld oder so.
Int: Wissen Sie, wie viele Ausländer in Deutschland leben?
Heiko: Weiß nicht genau. Ich glaube, 15% der Bevölkerung.
Int: Es sind 1,8%.
Heiko: Ist mir egal. Das sind immer noch zu viele.
Int: Welche Aktionen gegen Ausländer haben Sie schon unternommen?
Heiko: Wir haben die aus den Kneipen und Nachtlokalen in der Stadt rausgeworfen. Keiner darf mehr rein, sonst hat er mit uns zu rechnen.
Int: Ist es dabei zu Gewalttaten gekommen?
Heiko: Na, es gab am Anfang ein paar kleine Schlägereien, aber nichts Ernstes. Sie wehren sich nicht mehr. Sie wissen, dass es sich nicht lohnt.
Int: Sonst noch etwas?
Heiko: Mit der Freundin meiner Schwester habe ich gesprochen. Sie hatte was mit einem Türken. Das geht ja nicht – ein deutsches Mädel mit so einem.
Int: Hat sie die Beziehung abgebrochen?
Heiko: Ja, sie wusste, dass es für den Typen sonst schlecht aussehen würde.
Int: Glauben Sie, dass Sie das Recht haben, sich in das Leben anderer Menschen einzumischen?
Heiko: In so einem Fall ja. Das war nicht korrekt.
Int: Wären Sie bereit, schwerere Gewalttaten auszuüben, einen Angriff auf ein Asylantenheim zum Beispiel?
Heiko: Wenn es nicht anders ginge, ja. Ich hoffe, es würde nicht dazu kommen. Die Leute würden kein Asylantenheim in der Stadt tolerieren. Und ich möchte nicht unbedingt Probleme mit der Polizei, denn dadurch könnte ich meine Lehrstelle verlieren.

4 Students compose a letter to Heiko and try to convince him that his ideas are not right. Students' answers to activity 3 will help them with their letter.

5 In pairs students discuss:

a How do you explain the rise of the far-right in the former East Germany?
b What are the dangers of racism?
c How do you react to the fact that the far-right parties are gaining in popularity?
d How should violent racists be punished?
e What can the government do to help?

Prüfungstraining

Grammar and skills

- Using indirect speech
- The subjunctive
- Translating into German

Materials

- Students' Book pages 34–35
- Grammar Workbook page 69
- *Arbeitsblatt* 15

1 The text includes many examples of indirect speech. This first activity tests reading comprehension; students match the appropriate sentence halves.

Answers:
a 4 **b** 1 **c** 7 **d** 6 **e** 2 **f** 9 **g** 3 **h** 10 **i** 8 **j** 5 **k** 11

Grammatik

This section deals with reported speech in the subjunctive.

A Students pick out all the examples of the subjunctive from the text on page 34.

Answers:
lebe, sei, passiere, hätten reagiert, gebe, seien, tolerieren, wolle sich engagieren, hätten gehabt, sitze, anschneide, käme, behaupteten, seien, wegnähmen, habe sich verfestigt, sei, erzählten, seien, sei zu sehen, habe konfrontiert, hätten gehabt, seien, sei.

B Students now list the phrases from the text which introduce indirect speech.

Answers:
laut Markus; Jugendliche haben gesagt; Markus berichtet; Markus meint; Die Jugendlichen behaupteten; Jugendliche erzählten ihm; Er sagt

C Students select the subjunctives which have changed tense to show that they are in the subjunctive.

Answers:
die Schulen hätten im Großen und Ganzen positiv auf das Forum reagiert; hätten sie aber keine Möglichkeiten gehabt, positiv zu wirken; käme man; Die Jugendlichen behaupteten; die ihnen die Arbeitsplätze wegnähmen; Jugendlichen erzählten ihm; sie hätten Kontakt zu Menschen gehabt

D Students practise forming their own subjunctive sentences.

Answers:
a *Er sagte, das Forum wolle Rockkonzerte veranstalten.*
b *Er sagte, er habe das Forum vor drei Jahren gegründet.*
c *Er sagte, drei Schulen hätten bis jetzt an dem Projekt teilgenommen.*
d *Er sagte, das Forum unterscheide sich von anderen Initiativen.*

Tipp

A section to help students prepare for the translation into German which forms part of the exam.

A Students look in the text for vocabulary they could use to translate the sentence provided.

Answers:
Das Oranienburger Forum – sich spezialisierien auf – diskutieren – Rassismus – mit Schülern

B Students need to spot the different way that the German language translates sentences a–c in order to point out the possible mistakes they could make in translation.

Answers:
a *tense*
b *passive*
c *preposition; word order in relative clause*

C Students practise the tips they have learnt by translating the passage into German.

Suggested answer:
Das Oranienburger Forum gegen Rassismus spezialisiert sich auf Initiativen gegen Rechtsradikalismus in Schulen. Das Forum konfrontiert Schüler mit dem Problem von Rassismus, indem man Asylbewerber in die Schulen bringt und Vorurteile diskutiert. Videos werden auch gezeigt. Ein Ziel des Forums ist es, Gleichgültigkeit abzubauen und Schüler zu unterstützen, die sich aktiv engagieren wollen. Markus Kemper, Mitbegründer, glaubt, das Projekt sei erfolgreich gewesen. Größere Initiativen wie zum Beispiel Rockkonzerte werden jetzt durch finanzielle Hilfe vom Landkreis ermöglicht.

Zur Auswahl

Materials

- Students' Book page 36
- Solo CD, track 4
- Grammar Workbook page 69

1a Students read the accounts of the young people.

1b Students select the appropriate word from the box to fill each gap. Each word in the box will be used.

Answers:
a *gründen, Asylantenheim*
b *ermöglicht*
c *Atmosphäre*
d *kümmert sich*
e *Sprachkenntnissen*
f *bewundert, Erfahrungen*

2 Students work with a partner and use the photos as a stimulus to discuss the bulleted questions.

S

3 Students listen to two interviews (the first with an Italian, the second with a Greek) and answer the questions.

Answers:
Herr B.: *woher: Sizilien; seit wann: seit 35 Jahren; warum: keine Arbeit; Beruf: Restaurantbesitzer; Familie: italienische Frau, Kinder alle in Deutschland geboren, sprechen Deutsch und*

Italienisch; Einstellung: ein besseres Leben; Ausländerfeindlichkeit: nein

Herr J.: *woher: Griechenland; seit wann: seit 30 Jahren; warum: keine Arbeit; Beruf: Bauarbeiter; Familie: Frau Griechin, Kinder hier geboren; Einstellung: vermisst Griechenland, will zurück, aber die Kinder wollen hier bleiben; Ausländerfeindlichkeit: Bemerkungen auf der Straße, Probleme mit einem Jungen in der Schulklasse.*

p 36, activity 3

Interviewer:	Herr Bellanca, woher kommen Sie und wie lange leben Sie schon in Deutschland?
Herr Bellanca:	Ich bin vor 35 Jahren von Sizilien nach Deutschland gekommen.
Interviewer:	Und warum sind Sie gekommen?
Herr Bellanca:	Ja, in Sizilien gab es keine Arbeit, ich hatte nichts. Dann habe ich gehört, dass es möglich war, als Gastarbeiter nach Deutschland zu kommen.
Interviewer:	Und was haben Sie hier gemacht?
Herr Bellanca:	Ich habe zuerst in einer Fabrik gearbeitet und dann in einem italienischen Restaurant. Ich habe viel Geld gespart und jetzt habe ich mein eigenes Restaurant hier in der Innenstadt.
Interviewer:	Und haben Sie hier eine Familie gegründet?
Herr Bellanca:	Ja, meine Frau ist auch Italienerin. Die Kinder sind aber alle hier in Deutschland geboren. Sie sprechen Deutsch und Italienisch, aber sie sprechen eigentlich besser Deutsch.
Interviewer:	Sind Sie froh, dass Sie nach Deutschland gekommen sind?
Herr Bellanca:	Ja, sehr froh. Ich fahre zweimal im Jahr nach Italien, um meine Familie zu besuchen, aber ich will hier bleiben. Das Leben ist einfach besser – ich habe ein schönes Haus, ich verdiene gut.
Interviewer:	Haben Sie Probleme mit Ausländerfeindlichkeit gehabt?
Herr Bellanca:	Nein, die Kinder auch nicht. Wir haben deutsche Freunde, wir sind hier akzeptiert. Ich habe nie Probleme gehabt.

Interviewer:	Herr Jeronimidis, wie lange sind Sie schon in Deutschland?
Herr Jeronimidis:	Auch seit über dreißig Jahren.
Interviewer:	Und warum sind Sie gekommen?
Herr Jeronimidis:	Ich wollte Geld verdienen. In Griechenland habe ich keine Arbeit gefunden.
Interviewer:	Und was machen Sie hier?
Herr Jeronimidis:	Ich arbeite auf einer Baustelle. Ich arbeite seit dreißig Jahren dort. Ich muss bald eine andere Arbeit suchen – ich werde zu alt.
Interviewer:	Und haben Sie eine Familie hier?
Herr Jeronimidis:	Ja, meine Frau ist auch Griechin und die Kinder sind hier geboren.
Interviewer:	Sind Sie froh, dass Sie nach Deutschland gekommen sind?
Herr Jeronimidis:	Ja und nein. Ich bin froh, dass ich hier Arbeit habe, aber ich vermisse Griechenland sehr. Wenn ich in die Rente gehe, will ich nach Griechenland zurrückkehren. Das wird aber schwierig sein – die Kinder wollen hier bleiben.
Interviewer:	Haben Sie Probleme mit Ausländerfeindlichkeit gehabt?
Herr Jeronimidis:	Ja, schon. Bei der Arbeit ist alles kein Problem, die Kollegen kennen mich, aber manchmal hört man so blöde Bemerkungen auf der Straße. Mein Sohn hat auch ein paar Probleme mit einem anderen Jungen in seiner Klasse gehabt, aber ich glaube nicht, dass die meisten Deutschen uns hassen. Das sind nur ein paar Idioten.
Interviewer:	Danke für das Gespräch.

Armut und Reichtum Einheit 4

Unit objectives

By the end of this unit students will be able to:

- Compare poverty in Germany and in the Third World
- Discuss the problems of the homeless
- Talk about problems in the Third World and possible solutions

Grammar

By the end of this unit students will be able to:

- Use adjective endings
- Use cases

Skills

By the end of this unit students will be able to:

- Give opinions

Materials

- Students' Book page 37

Answers:

a 1 **b** 5 **c** 2 **d** 4 **e** 3

2a Students begin to think about the issues depicted above by writing answers to the questions a–d.

2b Draw together individual students' answers in a whole-class discussion on the topics introduced.

3 Students work in small groups to draw spidergrams with key words on the themes of *Armut* and *Reichtum*.

Armut in Deutschland

Materials

- Students' Book pages 38–39
- CD 1, track 14

1 As a class, discuss why so many German children are rely on social welfare today and compare this with the situation in the 1960s.

2a Students read the text.

2b Students find a word or sentence in the text for each of the definitions given.

Answers:

a *es lohnt sich nicht*
b *Beschäftigung*
c *Krach*
d *prügeln*
e *Teufelskreis*

2c Students choose the sentence that best matches the text.

Answers:

a 1 **b** 2 **c** 1 **d** 3 **e** 3 **f** 3 **g** 3

2d Students translate the last paragraph into English.

Answer:

For Gabi, life is even worse – rows with her mother and stepfather forced her to leave the parental home. She now lives on the streets. Here, she met Christoph. He has a similar story – his father beat him until he could bear no more. 'I wanted to find a job here in Munich', he says, 'but I gave up hope of that a long time ago. We are caught in a vicious circle. If you haven't got a permanent address, you can't get a job. Without a job you can't pay for accomodation. Nobody seems to care much about us. Of course there are hostels, especially in winter, but nobody is trying to get us out of this situation. The worst thing is neither the cold nor the filth. It is that you are treated like an animal. People who go by mostly don't look at you at all.'

3 Students listen to the report about BISS (*Bürger in sozialen Schwierigkeiten*) and answer questions a–h. Point out to students that BISS is the rough German equivalent of *Big Issue* in the UK.

Answers:

a *eine Zeitung*
b *der Chefredakteur*
c *Obdachlosen zu helfen; mehr Aufmerksamkeit auf die Schattenseiten einer reichen Industriegesellschaft zu lenken*
d *keine (Wir waren ein No-Budget Projekt)*
e *10 000 Exemplare des ersten Heftes waren nach wenigen Wochen weg; jetzt erscheint BISS alle zwei Monate mit einer Auflage von 50 000 Exemplaren*
f *Betrunken darf nicht verkauft werden und gleichzeitiges Betteln ist verboten.*
g *die Möglichkeit aus der Scham des Bettelns auszusteigen*
h *Jetzt versucht er wieder, etwas aus seinem Leben zu machen.*

p 39, activity 3

H.M.: Sie haben keinen Biss? Dann kaufen Sie sich einen Biss.

Int.: In der Münchener U-Bahn verkaufen Obdachlose ihre eigene Zeitung – BISS, abgekürzt für „Bürger in sozialen Schwierigkeiten". Chefredakteur Klaus Honigschnaben hat das Projekt ins Leben gerufen.

K.H.: Nicht eine Zeitung für Obdachlose wollten wir machen, sondern eine von und mit Obdachlosen.

Int.: Die Idee entstand am Rande einer Tagung der Evangelischen Akademie Tutzing. Das Anliegen war sowohl Obdachlosen konkret zu helfen, als auch mehr Aufmerksamkeit auf die Schattenseiten einer reichen Industriegesellschaft zu lenken.

K.H.: Wir waren ein No-Budget Projekt. Aber die 10 000 Exemplare des ersten Heftes waren nach wenigen Wochen weg.

Int.: Jetzt erscheint BISS alle zwei Monate mit einer Auflage von 50 000 Exemplaren. Die Zeitung wird von Obdachlosen verkauft, die vom Verkaufspreis von 75 Cent 50 Cent behalten dürfen. Dabei gelten feste Regeln: Betrunken darf nicht verkauft werden und gleichzeitiges Betteln ist verboten. Die Verkäufer gewinnen dadurch oft mehr als Geld. Für Hermann Merkl bedeutet die Zeitschrift die Möglichkeit, aus der Scham des Bettelns auszusteigen.

H.M.: Es ist ein großer Unterschied, ob du die Leute um Geld bittest, oder ob du Ihnen was verkaufst. Man hat ein ganz anderes Selbstwertgefühl. Seitdem ich BISS verkaufe, geht die Spirale wieder nach oben. Jetzt versuche ich wieder, etwas aus meinem Leben zu machen.

4 Students take part in a role-play. A plays the part of a journalist and B plays the part of a homeless person. They should cover the following points: how and why B became homeless, what B lives on, a typical day, help available, future plans.

5 Students imagine they are homeless and write an article of about 150 words for the newspaper BISS. This could be done for homework. Encourage them to use the vocabulary and ideas they have met on these pages in their writing.

Die Dritte Welt

Grammar focus

- Adjective endings

Materials

- Students' Book pages 40–41
- CD 1, track 15
- *Arbeitsblatt* 16
- Grammar Workbook pages 22–25

1 Students discuss with a partner which countries are part of the Third World and what problems these countries face. Draw these ideas together in a whole-class discussion.

2a After reading the text, students pick out the words which match the definitions a–f.

Answers:

a *Armut*
b *lebensnotwendig*
c *Analphabet*
d *Bürgerkrieg*
e *Dürren*
f *Hungersnöte*

2b Students write a list of the main problems facing Third World countries.

Suggested answers:

Armut, niedrige Lebenserwartung, wenige Ärzte, mangelnde Hygiene, geringe Bodenschätze, Überbevölkerung, unzureichende Nahrungsmittel, einen hohen Prozentsatz an Analphabetentum, wenige Schulen und Krankenhäuser, Krankheiten, wenig sauberes Wasser, Aids, manchmal: Bürgerkreige, Naturkatastrophen

2c To test reading comprehension, students complete the sentences with the appropriate ending.

Answers:

a *...fehlt es einem selbst an den dringend lebensnotwendigen Dingen.*
b *...dass er 40 Jahre leben wird. (or similar)*
c *...lesen noch schreiben.*
d *...breiten sich Krankheiten schnell aus.*
e *...werden finanzielle Mittel in Waffen gesteckt.*
f *...Naturkatastrophen wie Dürren oder Hungersnöte eintreten.*
g *...sie den Industrieländern Geld schulden.*
h *...14 Millionen Menschen.*

Grammatik

A Students pick out all the adjectives from the text and explain each ending (or no ending).

Answers:

der so genannten Dritten Welt = feminine singular, definite article, dative case

in absoluter Armut = feminine singular, no article, dative case

an den dringend lebensnotwendigen Dingen = plural, definite article, dative case

ist zu gering = stands alone, no ending

ist drastisch = stands alone, no ending

mangelnde Hygiene = feminine singular, no article, accusative case

geringe Bodensätze = plural, no article, accusative case

unzureichende Nahrungsmittel = plural, no article, accusative case

einen hohen Prozentsatz = masculine singular, indefinite article, accusative case

zu sauberem Wasser = neuter singular, no article, dative case

finanzielle Mittel = plural, no article, nominative case

auf internationale Hilfsorganisationen = plural, no article, accusative case

als tragisch = stands alone, no article

dem neuesten Problem = neuter, definite article, dative case in apposition to 'Aids'

B Students fill in the gaps with the appropriate adjective ending.

Answers:

a *häufige*
b *schwangeren*
c *nächsten*
d *schweren, weitflächigen*
e *armen, richtige*

3 Students listen to a report about child labour in the Third World and answer questions a–i.

Answers:

a *Teppichknüpfer, Hausmädchen, Prostituierte*
b *billige Arbeitskräfte*
c *25%*
d *weil die Familie es sich nicht mehr leisten kann, sie zu behalten*
e *In vielen Ländern müssen Kinder arbeiten, um die Familie zu ernähren.*
f *Kleinen Kindern werden noch kleinere Geschwister aufgebürdet, weil die Eltern sich Arbeit außer Haus suchen.*
g *Omar lernt jetzt den Beruf eines Fischers*
h *Omar will arbeiten und Geld verdienen. Er fühlt sich frei.*
i *Es behindert sowohl die Entwicklung der Kinder als auch des Landes.*

p 41, activity 3

Der Inder Schanker ist Teppichknüpfer, Sunita aus Nepal Hausmädchen, Daya Prostituierte in einem Bordell in Neu-Delhi. Alle drei sind noch Kinder, sechs, zehn und vierzehn Jahre alt, und werden als billige Arbeitskräfte ausgebeutet. Jedes vierte Kind zwischen funf und vierzehn Jahren muss arbeiten, rund 250 Millionen Kinder weltweit schätzt die Internationale Arbeitsorganisation. In manchen asiatischen Ländern werden Zwölfjährige an Bordelle verkauft, weil die Familie es sich nicht mehr leisten kann, sie zu behalten. In vielen Ländern müssen Kinder arbeiten, um die Familie zu ernähren. Kleinen Kindern werden noch kleinere Geschwister aufgebürdet, weil die Eltern sich Arbeit außer Haus suchen, andere müssen Arbeit in Bergwerken, Fabriken oder auf der Straße finden, um zum Familieneinkommen beizutragen. Nicht alle Kinder halten es für schlecht. Omar ist zehn Jahre alt und wohnt in Dakar. Er lernt jetzt den Beruf eines Fischers. Er geht jeden Morgen mit seinem Vater zum Fluss. Der Fang wird von der Mutter auf dem Markt verkauft. Omar hat keine Lust mehr auf die Schule – er will arbeiten und Geld verdienen. Er fühlt sich frei. Seine Arbeit mag wohl keine richtige Ausbeutung sein, aber es behindert sowohl die Entwicklung der Kinder als auch des Landes. In Senegal können nur 30% der Bevölkerung lesen und schreiben.

4 Students research a Third-World country in order to prepare to give a talk about it to the class. Bullet points are given to focus their preparation, and they should also make use of the *Hilfe* on the page.

Extra! Students use the information from activity 4 to write a report on a country of their choice.

Extra! Students listen to the recording and answer the questions on copymaster 16.

A 16

Kampf gegen Armut

Key language

- *die Dritte Welt unterstützen*

- *zur nachhaltigen Entwicklung beitragen*
- *bessere Lebensbedingungen verschaffen*
- *fairen Handel versichern*
- *langfristige Probleme lösen*

Materials

- Students' Book pages 42–43
- CD 1, track 17
- *Arbeitsblatt* 17

1 Students discuss the list of questions with a partner.

2a Students read the text.

2b Students read through the text again and find the German for the words listed.

Answers:

a *Wohlfahrtsorganisationen*
b *langfristig*
c *nachhaltige Entwicklung*
d *lindern*
e *handeln*
f *Ernte*
g *dementsprechend*

2c Students decide whether the sentences are true (R), false (F) or not mentioned in the text (N).

Answers:

a R **b** R **c** N **d** F **e** R **f** R **g** F **h** F

3 Students design an advertisement for fairtrade products. Encourage them to use the vocabulary listed in the *Hilfe* box and to draw upon the ideas presented on these pages.

4 Students listen to the report and answer the questions in German.

Answers:

a *Er war ausgebildeter Lehrer, mit fünf Jahren Erfahrung.*
b *Er war sehr beeindruckt von dem, was er sah.*
c *Die Regierung will immer mehr Kinder einschulen und es gibt nicht genug Lehrer.*
d *Lehrpläne entwickeln und für Fortbildung verantwortlich sein*
e *ein Weg aus der Armut*
f *wie eifrig die Kinder sind*
g *Schüler in Afrika wollen unbedingt lernen. / In Deutschland haben sie oft keinen Bock.*
h *Er schämt sich.*

p 43, activity 4

Ich war schon ausgebildeter Lehrer und hatte fünf Jahre Erfahrung in einer Realschule in Deutschland, als ich mich entschied, in den Sommerferien nach Afrika zu fahren. Ich habe mich zuerst für einen kurzfristigen Aufenthalt entschieden, war aber so beeindruckt, dass ich dann für zwei Jahre blieb. Als Lehrer in Äthiopien kann man direkt helfen. Es gibt nicht genug Lehrer und die Regierung versucht, immer mehr Kinder einzuschulen. Ich habe zuerst ein Jahr in einer Schule gearbeitet und dann eine Stelle als Beratungslehrer bekommen. Ich habe in anderen Schulen geholfen, Lehrpläne zu entwickeln, und war für Fortbildung verantwortlich. Für Leute in Äthiopien ist eine gute Ausbildung ein Weg aus der Armut. Und das Land braucht besser informierte Bürger, um Fortschritte zu machen. Am meisten hat mir imponiert, wie eifrig die Kinder dort sind. Viele gehen jeden Tag Kilometer zu Fuß, um in die Schule zu kommen. Sie wollen unbedingt lernen. Wenn ich sie mit Schülern in Deutschland vergleiche, die oft keinen Bock haben, schäme ich mich.

5 Students research a charity of their choice and write a report about its work. Some useful websites are given in the Students' Book for German charities which students could research.

6 Students work with a partner to discuss the questions listed. Encourage them to draw upon the vocabulary and ideas presented on these pages in their discussions.

Prüfungstraining

Grammar and skills

- Revising adjective endings and cases
- Giving opinions
- *Arbeitsblatt* 20

Materials

- Students' Book pages 44–45
- Grammar Workbook pages 10–18, 22–24

1 Students read the text and fill in the gaps with the correct adjective endings and articles.

Answers:

*Seit anderthalb Jahren ist Gabi Kortmann mit ihr**em** Kollegen Karl Eiter für **die** deutsche Gesellschalft für technische Zusammenarbeit in Malawi im Einsatz. Ihre Aufgabe: **den** Gesundheitsdienst im Bezirk Chipita zu unterstützen. Im ganz**en** Bezirk leben 135 000 Leute und für **alle diese** Menschen gibt es nur ein einzig**es** Krankenhaus mit 120 Betten. Gabi und Karl sind **die** einzig**en** Ärzte.*

*Ein malawisch**er** Arzt hat noch nie hier gearbeitet. Kein**er** will dies**en** Job. **Das** Land ist arm, **das** Gehalt miserabel, **die** Lebens- und Arbeitszustände sind* *katastrophal. Bei Regen ist **die** Verbindungsstraße zum Rest **der** Welt unbefahrbar. Strom, Benzin und Paraffin sind Glückssache. Im Krankenhaus mangelt es an all**em**: an Hygiene, heiß**em** Wasser, Medikamenten und Personal.*

*Nur eines gibt es im Überfluss: Patienten. In Malawi stirbt jed**es** 10. Kind bei **der** Geburt. **Die** durchschnittlich**e** Lebenserwartung liegt bei 38 Jahren. Jed**er** Dritt**e** hat Aids. Warum will **die** ehemalig**e** Oberärztin hier arbeiten? „Im Urlaub haben Karl und ich wiederholt in **der** Dritt**en** Welt gearbeitet", erklärt sie. „Hier habe ich halb verhungert**e** Kinder gesehen und in ein**em** Flüchtlingslager gearbeitet. **Die** Probleme in Deutschland schienen wie nichts dagegen." Schließlich wurde **der** Entschluss gefasst, Deutschland zu verlassen und Nothilfe im Ausland zu leisten. **Die** beid**en** kündigten.*

2a Students read the text on page 44 and pick out the German equivalents of the English vocabulary listed (a–e).

Answers:

a *im Einsatz*
b *Arbeitszustände*
c *es mangelt an allem*
d *Überfluss*
e *wiederholt*

2b To test reading comprehension, students decide whether each sentence (a–i) is true (R), false (F) or not mentioned in the text (N).

Answers:

a *R*
b *N*
c *R*
d *R*
e *F (es mangelt an allem: an ... Medikamenten ...)*
f *F (nur eines gibt es im Überfluss: Patienten)*
g R
h *N*
i *F (Die beiden kündigten, um Nothilfe im Ausland zu leisten.)*

2c Students imagine they are Gabi Kortmann and write an account of her life and work in Africa. The bullet points can be used as a guide to what students should include.

Grammatik

A Students make sure they are confident in using the different cases in German as well as their corresponding adjective endings by checking they can answer the questions listed.

B Students use each of the prepositions listed in a sentence related to the theme of poverty.

Tipp

3 Students read the text and in pairs discuss whether they agree with Gabi Kortmann when she says that the problems in Germany are nothing compared with those in the Third World. They should use the information in the *Tipp* box to help them.

4 The class has a debate on the topic of spending money on the Third World when there are many problems at home. They should use the information in the *Tipp* box to help them.

Zur Auswahl

Materials

- Students' Book page 46
- Solo CD, track 5
- *Arbeitsblatt* 18

1 Students listen to a report about the work of the *deutsche Kinderschutzbund* and then choose the appropriate ending for each sentence (a–g).

Answers:

a 1 **b** 3 **c** 2 **d** 2 **e** 2 **f** 3 **g** 3

p 46, activity 1

Int.: Der deutsche Kinderschutzbund setzt sich für die Interessen von Kindern in der Bundesrepublik ein. Die Grundlage für alle Aktivitäten der Organisation ist die UN-Konvention über die Rechte des Kindes. Die zwei zentralen Arbeitsbereiche des Bundes betreffen Kinder, die in Armut leben, und Kinder, die Opfer von Gewalt sind. Die Aktivitäten des Bundes sind vielseitig. Johanna ist neun Monate alt und liegt mit Brüchen im Krankenhaus. Der Arzt ruft Nicole an, eine Beraterin vom Kinderschutzbund. Für sie gehören solche Fälle zum Alltag. Sie arrangiert ein Treffen mit den Eltern. Beide sind unter 20, lieben ihr Kind, sind aber hilflos, verzweifelt, kommen mit ihrer Elternrolle nicht klar. Der Grundsatz der Organisation heißt „Hilfe statt Strafe". Dazu Nicole:

N.:	Um das Kind vor weiterer Gewalt zu schützen, muss man den Eltern eigentlich Hilfe gewähren.
Int.:	Zuerst bleibt Johanna im Krankenhaus, dann wird mit den Eltern zusammen geplant, wie es weiter gehen soll.
N.:	Zuerst müssen wir den Auslöser für die Gewalt finden. Oft wurden gewalttätige Eltern selber während ihrer Kindheit geschlagen. Es ist wichtig, einen Weg aus diesem Teufelskreis zu finden.
Int.:	In armen Innenstädten bietet der Bund Spielmobile und Eltern-Treff-Gruppen an. Der Bund finanziert auch das Kinder- und Jugendtelefon, die so genannte „Nummer gegen Kummer". Rund 10 000 Mädchen und Jungen rufen täglich die kostenfreie Nummer an, um mit einem Berater über Probleme zu sprechen. Thema Nummer 1 ist Liebe und Sexualität, aber es melden sich auch Kinder, die sexuellen Missbrauch oder Gewalt zu Haus erlitten haben, und sonst keinen Ansprechpartner haben. Im politischen Bereich ist der Kinderschutzbund auch aktiv. Die Organisation sieht sich als Lobby für Kinder. Die führende Kampagne im Moment – Kinderpornographie im Internet.

2 Students discuss questions a–h with a partner to revise the themes of poverty, charity and the Third World.

3 Students choose three of the questions from activity 2 and write up their answers. This could be done for homework.

4 Students translate the German sentences into English.

Answers:

a *The German Child Protection Society supports the interests of children in the Federal Republic. The basis for all the organisation's activities is the UN convention of the rights of children. The society's two main areas of work are children living in poverty and children who are the victims of violence.*

b *The mission was both to help the homeless and in a concrete way and to draw more attention to the dark side of a rich industrial society.*

c *What is seen as tragic in the First World is an everyday occurrence in developing countries.*

Wiederholung Einheit 3–4

Materials

- Students' Book, pages 47–48
- CD 1, tracks 18–19
- *Arbeitsblatt* 19

1 Students read the text about nationality and then translate it.

Possible answer:

Many immigrant workers and their families have lived in Germany for twenty years. The children were often born here. They work here and pay taxes but are not allowed to vote, because they are still foreign citizens. Foreigners who live in Germany for longer and fulfil certain conditions can apply for German nationality. Only 1.1% of the foreign population have done so, however. The reason: they have to give up their old nationality. Not many of the older generation are willing to do this. And the second generation often do not want to offend their parents by giving up their old homeland. So is dual nationality the only solution?

2a Students listen to four people's opinions on dual nationality.

2b Students attribute each of the sentences (a–f) to the appropriate person.

Answers:

a *Marianne*
b *Karin*
c *Peter*
d *Cornelius*
e *Marianne*
f *Karin*

p 47, activities 2a and 2b

Marianne:	Ich habe nichts gegen die doppelte Staatsbürgerschaft. Die Gastarbeiter haben viel zu der deutschen Gesellschaft beigetragen. Sie zahlen auch sehr viel in die Rentenkasse und an Steuern. Es ist eine Schande, dass sie kein volles Wahlrecht haben.
Peter:	Man soll sich für ein Land entscheiden – man kann nicht zwei haben. Das finde ich ungerecht.
Cornelius:	Ich glaube, es ist eine Identitätsfrage. Für die zweite Generation, die in Deutschland geboren ist, ist das sowieso sehr schwierig. Ich habe mehrere Freunde aus Ausländerfamilien, die in Deutschland

	bleiben wollen. Aber sie fühlen sich zwischen zwei Welten hin- und hergerissen. Die doppelte Staatsbürgerschaft würde ihnen vielleicht helfen, sich hier wohler zu fühlen.
Karin:	Die doppelte Staatsbürgerschaft bringt viele Probleme mit sich. Wie ist es, wenn die beiden Länder ganz andere Gesetze haben? Und wo soll man Wehrdienst leisten? Ich glaube, es würde immer wieder Fälle geben, wo man zwischen den beiden Ländern entscheiden müsste. Es ist besser, das nur einmal zu machen, und sich für einen Staat zu entscheiden.

3 A whole-class debate about whether dual nationality should be allowed.

4 In pairs, students discuss the following questions:

- **a** What do you know about racism in Germany during the Second World War?
- **b** Which groups of foreigners came to Germany after the war?
- **c** Which other foreigners live in Germany?
- **d** What do you know about racism in Germany today?
- **e** Why is racism worse in the new *Bundesländer*?
- **f** What do you think are the causes of racism?
- **g** Give examples of projects or events which try to fight racism.
- **h** Which other countries have problems with racism?
- **i** What do you know about far-right parties in Europe?
- **j** In which countries are these parties influential?

5 Students listen to the report about a Romanian orphanage and answer questions a–h.

Answers:

- **a** *im Kinderheim im Rumänien*
- **b** *sechs Kinder und drei Betreuer*
- **c** *schwer traumatisiert, abgemagert und mit motorischen Störungen*
- **d** *liebevolle Betreuer, besseres Essen, können im Freien und mit Tieren spielen*
- **e** *Heimkinder bekommen 7000 Lei pro Tag von der Gemeindeverwaltung. Das reicht gerade für eine Brotration. Und selbst dieses Geld wird nicht immer bezahlt.*
- **f** *Spenden*
- **g** *Nahrungsmittel, Medikamente, warme Kleidung und auch Spielzeuge für die Kinder*
- **h** *fehlendes Personal*

p 48, activity 5

André und Attila wohnten bis vor drei Jahren im Kinderheim von Bradca in Rumänien. Sie hatten aber Glück. Die englische Hilfsorganisation „White Cross" richtete drei Bauernhöfe in der Umgebung her und holte 18 Kinder aus dem Heim. Seitdem wohnen die beiden zusammen mit vier anderen Kindern und drei Betreuern auf einem von diesen Höfen. „Als sie ankamen, waren sie schwer traumatisiert, abgemagert und hatten motorische Störungen", erinnert sich Roger Heimer, ein Helfer von White Cross. Ganz langsam gelang es den Betreuern an die beiden heranzukommen, so dass sie sich ihnen gegenüber öffneten. Heute spielen die beiden auf dem Hof, füttern die Schweine. Lachend rennen sie zum Abendessen. Solche Erfolgsgeschichten sind selten in Rumänien. Kaum ein Heimkind hat das Glück, von liebevollen Menschen betreut zu werden. Heimkinder bekommen 7000 Lei pro Tag von der Gemeindeverwaltung. Das reicht gerade für eine Brotration. Und selbst dieses Geld wird nicht immer bezahlt. Ohne Spenden wären die Heime verloren. Hilfsgüter kommen aus Deutschland und anderen europäischen Ländern. Nahrungsmittel, Medikamente, warme Kleidung und auch Spielzeuge für die Kinder werden in Lastwagen transportiert. So wird für die dringendsten Bedürfnisse dieser Kinder gesorgt. Sie verhungern nicht, sie erfrieren nicht, aber eine richtige Kindheit haben sie auch nicht. Fehlendes Personal schließt die Möglichkeit, die psychischen Probleme der Kinder zu lösen aus. Viel mehr Geld wird gebraucht, um weitere Heime wie die White Cross Bauernhöfe einzurichten, und den Kindern damit ein richtiges Zuhause zu geben.

6a Students read the article.

6b Students read the eight statements and then decide which are true (R), which are false (F) and which aren't mentioned (N).

Answers:

- **a** *R*
- **b** *F – Die Probleme sind keineswegs mit denen der Dritten Welt vergleichbar.*
- **c** *R*
- **d** *R*
- **e** *N*
- **f** *F – Dazu kann auch Neid kommen – or Arme Kinder sind (oft) eifersüchtig auf ...*
- **g** *N*
- **h** *R*

7 Students translate the sentences into German.

Answers:

a *Obwohl die Situation in Deutschland keinesweg mit der Lage in der Dritten Welt vergleichbar ist, ist Armut ein echtes Problem.*

b *Armut hat auch schlimme Folgen für die Kinder, was ihre Entwicklung betrifft.*

c *Kinder, die unter der Armutsgrenze aufwachsen, fühlen sich oft minderwertig.*

d *Es ist höchstwahrscheinlich, dass Kinder aus armen Familien Verbrechen begehen werden.*

Rechtswesen und Verbrechen Einheit 5

Unit objectives

By the end of this unit students will be able to:

- Discuss reasons for youth crime and antisocial behaviour
- Discuss the problems of Internet crime
- Discuss the importance and the effect of media coverage on crime
- Discuss measures to reduce crime and express an opinion about their effectiveness

Grammar

By the end of this unit students will be able to:

- Use modal verbs and *lassen*
- Use verbs of perception

Skills

By the end of this unit students will be able to:

- Defend a point of view

Materials

Student's Book page 49

1a Students look at the pictures and consider why young people commit crimes. Are there any other reasons they can think of?

1b Which crimes are being portrayed here? Students should use a dictionary to find the exact terms for these crimes.

Jugendkriminalität

Skills focus

- Translating into German

Materials

- Students' Book pages 50–51
- CD 1, track 20
- *Arbeitsblätter* 21, 22, 23

1 Students look at the chart and see how the number of criminal offences has changed between 1998 und 2006. They then say which age group commits the most crimes.

2a Students read the text, *Begehen Jugendliche immer mehr Straftaten?*.

2b Students find the German phrases in the text that correspond with the English phrases listed.

Answers:

a *Tatverdächtige*
b *Straftat*
c *erfassen*
d *verurteilt*
e *Sachbeschädigung*
f *Opfer*
g *scheinen*
h *Gewaltverbrechen/Gewalttaten*
i *benachrichtigen*
j *Gerichtsverfahren*

2c Students read through the text again and find synonyms for the words listed.

Answers:

a *betrachtet man*
b *Straftaten*
c *gleichaltrig*
d *ans Tageslicht kommen*
e *Täter, Delinquenten*

2d Students read through once more and answer the questions in order to test comprehension.

Answers:

a *Ab 20 geht die Zahl der Tatverdächtigen zurück.*
b *wie viele Straftäter verurteilt wurden*
c *Ladendiebstahl, Sachbeschädigung oder Schwarzfahren*
d *gegen Gleichaltrige*
e *Es erfolgten mehr Anzeigen, die Polizei wurde häufiger benachrichtigt und die Behörden und die Öffentlichkeit sind aufmerksamer.*

3 Students translate the sentences into German. Refer them to the *Tipp* on page 35 of the Students' Book for support.

Answers:

a *Junge Straftäter scheinen meist leichte Delikte zu begehen.*
b *Bei einem Viertel/25 Prozent aller jugendlichen Verbrechen handelt es sich um Körperverletzung.*
c *Studien in mehreren deutschen Städten haben gezeigt, dass die Zahl der Gewaltverbrechen gesunken ist.*

d *Die Öffentlichkeit ist aufmerksamer und die Polizei wird häufiger benachrichtigt.*

4a Students match the German and English phrases.

Answers:
a 2 **b** 4 **c** 5 **d** 6 **e** 1 **f** 3

4b Students listen to a report about youth crime. They then decide which sentences are true (R) and which are false (F). They correct any that are false.

Answers:
- **a** *R*
- **b** *F – Gewalttätige Eltern haben **oft** gewalttätige Kinder.*
- **c** *F – Der Sicherheitsbericht der Bundesregierung sagt, dass zugewanderte Jugendliche sich nicht akzeptiert fühlen.*
- **d** *F – Zugewanderte Familien haben manchmal eine andere Einstellung zu Männlichkeit und Ehre.*
- **e** *Der Aufenthaltsstatus spielt oft **eine** Rolle.*
- **f** *R*

p 51, activities 4b and 4c

Sowohl Heranwachsende als auch junge Erwachsene weisen eine relativ hohe Kriminalitätsbelastung auf. Gefährdet sind Jugendliche mit geringem Selbstwertgefühl und ohne Zukunftsperspektive, aber vor allem auch junge Menschen, die aus sozial benachteiligten Familien oder einem Elternhaus kommen, in dem die Eltern ihre Kinder schlagen. Das soziale Umfeld spielt also eine große Rolle bei der Entwicklung von Aggression, denn Opfer von aggressiven, gewalttätigen Eltern werden oft selbst zu Tätern.

Bei ausländischen Jugendlichen der zweiten und dritten Generation liegt aus ähnlichen Gründen eine höhere Kriminalitätsbelastung vor. Dazu kommt noch, so der Sicherheitsbericht der Bundesregierung, dass diese Jugendlichen sich nicht akzeptiert und gleich behandelt fühlen. Diese Erfahrung sehen sie als Diskriminierung an, und das kann zu Konflikthaltungen führen. Zugewanderte Familien haben auch manchmal andere Vorstellungen von Männlichkeit und Ehre, was ebenfalls ein Faktor sein kann.

Bei manchen ausländischen Jugendlichen kann es auch zu einer höheren Kriminalitätsbelastung kommen, wenn ihr Aufenthaltsstatus nicht sicher ist und sie keine permanente Aufenthaltsgenehmigung haben.

Eine aktive Integrationspolitik für Jugendliche am Rande unserer Gesellschaft ist also eine wichtige Voraussetzung für einen Rückgang der Jugendkriminalität. Junge Heranwachsende brauchen ein Ziel, etwas, das ihr Leben lebenswert macht.

4c Students listen to the report again and make notes on the points listed.

5 Students perform a role-play with a partner. Each partner thinks about a relevant question on the topic of youth crime and works on an answer. They should use the text, *Begehen Jugendliche immer mehr Straftaten?* on page 50 of the Students' Book and the listening text from activity 4 for ideas. Partner A plays the interviewer and B, an expert in youth crime.

6 Students prepare a PowerPoint presentation on the topic of youth crime. They should mention the points listed.

Internetkriminalität

Key language
- *Es gibt sowohl ... als auch ...*
- *Betrachtet man zuerst die Vorteile, so sieht man, dass ...*
- *Die Vorteile sind offensichtlich/eindeutig.*
- *Es gibt überwiegend ...*
- *Es hängt davon ab, ... (ob, inwieweit) ...*
- *Es kommt auf ... an.*
- *Es kommt darauf an, ... (ob, inwieweit) ...*
- *Man darf auch nicht vergessen, dass ...*

Materials
- Students' Book pages 52–53
- CD 1, track 21

1 Students discuss what they understand by the term Internet crime. They give some examples.

2a Students match the definitions and synonyms to the expressions listed.

Answers:
a 6 **b** 4 **c** 1 **d** 5 **e** 2 **f** 3

2b Students read the interview with an expert on Internet crime.

2c Students complete the sentences with the most appropriate word or phrase.

Answers:
a 3 **b** 1 **c** 1 **d** 2 **e** 2

3 Students read the newspaper headings. First they look up any unknown words in a dictionary. They then discuss as a class what they think of the way in which the media reports on crime.

4a Students listen to a discussion between four young people about crime and media reporting. They then decide which of the opinions listed are mentioned in the discussion and whose opinions they are.

Answers:

a – Olli, c – Katrin, d– Susi, e– Lutz, g– Katrin, h – Susi

p 53, activities 4a and 4b

Katrin:	Hallo! Habt ihr heute schon die Zeitung gelesen? Es gibt da wieder ein paar knallharte Überschriften. Ich kann es einfach nicht ausstehen, wenn Reporter so sensationell über alles berichten. Es geht ihnen gar nicht um die Leute, über die sie schreiben, sondern nur darum, möglichst viele Zeitungsexemplare zu verkaufen. Was meinst du, Olli?
Olli:	Teilweise muss ich dir schon Recht geben, Katrin. Natürlich wollen und müssen sie ihre Artikel verkaufen, denn davon leben sie ja. Meiner Ansicht nach ist es aber die Pflicht eines Journalisten, nicht nur über Politik, sondern auch über Verbrechen and anderes zu berichten. Wie stehst du dazu, Lutz?
Lutz:	Ich halte es vor allem für wichtig, dass die Reporter die Wahrheit berichten und nicht so total übertreiben, dass ein ganz anderes Bild entsteht. Das kommt bei Artikeln über Kriminalität zu oft vor, und dann wird die Information verfälscht und die Leser machen sich ein total falsches Bild von einem Ereignis. Susi, du hast noch nichts gesagt. Was meinst du dazu?
Susi:	Ich bin der Auffassung, Zeitungsberichterstatter sollen, ja, sie müssen sogar interessante Artikel schreiben können, erst dann lesen die Leser sie mit Interesse. Und wenn sie dabei ab und zu übertreiben, ist das doch nicht schlimm. Ich lese diese Artikel gern. Sie sind viel leichter zu verstehen. Meiner Meinung nach ist es die Pflicht der Reporter, Bericht zu erstatten, und wie sie das machen ist ihre Sache.

4b Students listen to the discussion once more and note down exactly what each of the young people says in order to express their opinion. There are six different phrases.

Answers:
Ich kann es einfach nicht ausstehen/Teilweise muss ich dir schon Recht geben/Meiner Ansicht nach/Ich halte es vor allem für wichtig/Ich bin der Auffassung/Meiner Meinung nach ist es…

4c Students write a summary on the topic of crime and how the media reports on it. They should include their opinion on this topic and write about 200 words. Encourage them to use some of the phrases from activity 5b as well as the *Hilfe* box on page 55.

Bewährungshilfe, Gefängnis oder gar Todesstrafe?

Materials

- Students' Book pages 54–55
- CD 1, track 22

1a Students look at the pictures and think about the various punishments portrayed. They list the crimes and criminal offences that have been mentioned in this unit so far. They then work with a partner and think about which punishment they consider to be appropriate for which crime.

1b Students read the statements and think about which ones they agree with and why. They then discuss this as a class.

1c Students choose the statements with which they least agree and work on counter-arguments for these. They then discuss this as a class.

1d Students read the opinions and note down with which of the statements from activity 1b they agree.

Answers:

Frauke: c; Sam: b; Marie: e; Stefan: f

2a Students listen to the report.

p 55, activities 2a,2b and 2c

In Nordrhein-Westfalen wurde vor einigen Monaten das erste Erziehungscamp des Bundeslandes eingerichtet. Die Einrichtung ist zunächst für acht Kinder beziehungsweise junge Jugendliche zwischen 12 und 15 Jahren gedacht. Das Ziel des Erziehungscamps ist es, diese jungen Menschen, die bereits straffällig geworden sind, zu betreuen und sie durch Sport, Disziplin, Arbeit und strenge Regeln wieder in die Gesellschaft zurückzuführen. Dabei steht aber auch Verhaltenstraining im Mittelpunkt. Die Jugendlichen sollen lernen, ohne Aggressionen in Konfliktsituationen zu reagieren. Man will also nicht die US- Camps für jugendliche Straftäter als Vorbild nehmen, denn dort werden Jugendliche oft gedemütigt.

Das Projekt wird von der Kaiserswerther Jugendhilfe getragen. In einer späteren Phase soll die Einrichtung auch für ältere jugendliche Straftäter ausgebaut werden.

Außerdem will die nordrhein-westfälische Landesregierung es durch weitere Maßnahmen ergänzen, die dazu beitragen sollen, gegen Jugendkriminalität anzugehen. Täter zwischen 18 und 21 Jahren sollen jedoch nach dem Erwachsenenstrafrecht bestraft werden.

[from: www.wdr.de/themen/panorama/kriminalitaet, Donnerstag,10.04.08]

2b Students read the statements and decide whether they are true (R), false (F) or not mentioned (N).

Answers:

a *F – In Nordrhein-Westfalen wurde vor einigen Monaten das erste Erziehungscamp des Bundeslands eingerichtet.*

b *F – Ziel ist es, straffälligen Jugendlichen zu helfen.*

c *N*

d *R*

e *F – Man will den Jugendlichen durch Sport, Disziplin, Arbeit, strenge Regeln und auch durch Verhaltenstraining helfen.*

f *N*

2c Students listen to the report again and fill in the gaps.

Answers:

a *8, 12, 15*

b *Disziplin*

c *Konflikte, Aggression*

d *Maßnahmen*

e *Jugendkriminalität*

f *18, 21*

3a Students work with a partner to discuss the advantages and disadvantages of 'brat camps'. They then discuss this topic as a class.

3b Students try to defend their viewpoint on the topic of 'brat camps' in a class debate. Encourage them to use the ideas and vocabulary presented on these pages.

4 Students write an article outlining their opinions on the topic of combating crime effectively. They should use the phrases from page 53 of the Students' Book and the *Tipp* on page 57 of the Students' Book for support.

Prüfungstraining

Grammar and skills

- Using modal verbs, the verb *lassen* and verbs of perception in the perfect tense
- Defending a point of view
- *Arbeitsblätter* 24, 25

Materials

- Students' Book pages 56–57
- Grammar Workbook pages 52, 53, 80–81

Grammatik

A Students read the short text and note down the modal verbs.

Answers:

sollen, sollen, müssen, dürfen, kann, können

B Students look at the sentences in the perfect tense and translate them into English.

Answers:

a *The young offenders were supposed to have learnt how to live in a community without being aggressive.*

b *They had to stick rigidly to the rules.*

c *They weren't allowed to do simply what they just wanted to do.*

d *The eight-year-old boy was glad that he has never had to go to a proper prison.*

C Students choose the correct verb in the sentences.

Answers:

a *wollen*

b *gedurft*

c *können*

d *sollen*

e *gemusst*

D Students read the sentences and translate them into English.

Answers:

a *He gets the criminal locked up.*
b *The murderer let the weapon fall.*
c *With the reward, she has a house built.*
d *The sentence isn't easily changed.*

E Students match up the sentences.

Answers:

a 2 **b** 4 **c** 1 **d** 3

Tipp

A Students match the German and English phrases.

Answers:

a 4 **b** 4 **c** 2 **d** 5 **e** 1 **f** 3

1a Students read the text and discuss the case with a partner. They decide whether they think the sentence passed was just or not and how would they have judged it. They should give reasons for their opinions. Encourage them to use the phrases from the *Tipp* section.

1b A whole-class discussion on the case in 1a. Students should use the vocabulary from the *Tipp* section.

Zur Auswahl

Materials

- Students' Book page 58
- Solo CD, track 6
- Grammar Workbook page

S 

1 Students listen to the recording and answer the questions to test their comprehension.

Answers:

a *im Eingangsbereich eines Geschäftshauses*
b *Die Täter sind mit Stöcken und Golfschlägem auf die Männer losgegangen.*
c *es gelang einem der Opfer noch während des Überfalls mit seinem Handy die Polizei zu alarmieren*
d *ein 33-Jähriger, sein 68 Jahre alter Vater sowie zwei 35 und 57 Jahre alte Bekannte*

p 58, activity 1

Bei einem Überfall haben fünf Täter vier Männer schwer verletzt. Wie die Polizei berichtet, waren die Täter am Montagabend im Eingangsbereich eines Geschäftshauses mit Stöcken und Golfschlägern auf die Männer losgegangen. Schusswaffen wurden nicht eingesetzt. Glücklicherweise gelang es einem der Opfer noch während des Überfalls mit seinem Handy die Polizei zu alarmieren. Die Täter ergriffen die Flucht. Ein 33-Jähriger, sein 68 Jahre alter Vater sowie zwei 35 und 57 Jahre alte Bekannte wurden schwer verletzt.

2 A class discussion based on the picture and speech bubbles. Encourage students to use expressions from the *Tipp* section on page 57 of the Students' Book.

3 Students translate the sentences into German.

Answers:

a *Überwachungskameras sind eine wirkungsvolle Methode, da sie die Kriminalität in den Städten reduzieren können.*
b *Junge Menschen, die nicht in die Gesellschaft integriert sind, sind gefährdeter.*
c *Am 31. Mai 2008 fanden in mehreren deutschen Städten Demonstrationen gegen elektronische Überwachung statt.*
d *Wenn jeder Jugendliche Arbeit hätte, gäbe es weniger Gewalt und Verbrechen.*

4a Students read the text.

4b Students then complete the sentences.

Answers:

a *... gegen den vermehrten Einsatz von Überwachungskameras ....*
b *... Informationsveranstaltungen, Workshops und Kunstaktionen.*
c *... ein Wohnzimmer mitten in einer Fußgängerzone aufstellte.*
d *... mögliche Gefahren und Auswirkungen der elektronischen Überwachung aufgeklärt und informiert.*

Technik und die Zukunft
Einheit 6

Unit objectives

By the end of this unit students will be able to:

- Discuss the use of gene technology
- Talk about the role of technology in the work place
- Discuss progress made in medicine

Grammar

By the end of this unit students will be able to:

- Use the future perfect
- Use the conditional perfect
- Use the imperfect subjunctive

Skills

By the end of this unit students will be able to:

- Listen with comprehension

Materials

- Students' Book page 59

1a Go through the vocabulary in the sentences on the page and then ask students to list which ideas they think are realistic and which are not.

1b Broaden this into a whole-class discussion about what the future may hold.

Das Essen der Zukunft

Materials

- Students' Book pages 60–61
- CD 2, track 2

1 Look at the poster with students and discuss GM foods. Do students know any foods which are genetically modified and the reasons for genetic modification.

2a Read through the text with students and then find synonyms for the German words listed.

Answers:

a *faulen*
b *bestreiten*
c *prüfen*
d *herstellen*
e *vorteilhaft*
f *skeptisch*

2b A true/false activity to test reading comprehension.

Answers:

a R
b R
c F – *Die Hauptangst der Deutschen ist, dass man sich mit der Gentechnik zu sehr in die Natur einmischt.*
d R
e F – *Die Gentechnik könnte den Welthunger stillen.*
f F – *Sie ist skeptisch.*
g R

2c Ask students to make a list of the pros and cons of GM foods.

Answers:

Vorteile: *Obst und Gemüse faulen nicht so schnell. Es wird vielleicht möglich sein, Krankheiten mit genmanipulierten Produkten zu heilen. Man wird vielleicht den Welthunger stillen können, indem man hitzeresistente Getreidesorten enwickelt.*

Nachteile: *Es kann gefährlich sein, sich in die Natur einzumischen (z.B. BSE). Die Folgen sind unsicher – neue Allergien sind eine Möglichkeit.*

3a Two young people give their views on GM foods. Students pick the sentence which best sums up Dieter's and Nathalie's views.

Answers:

Dieter: b Nathalie: e

p 61, activities 3a and 3b

D.: Ich habe keine Probleme damit, dass gentechnisch veränderte Lebensmittel entwickelt werden. Durch sie wird es möglich, Lebensmittel in trockeneren Gegenden der Erde anzubauen. Außerdem könnte man Kühe so verändern, dass sie mehr Milch liefern, und wichtige Nährstoffe wie Vitamine und Ballaststoffe in größeren Mengen in Nahrungsmittel einführen. Angesichts der 830 Millionen unterernährten Menschen in den Entwicklungsländern, wäre es eine Schande, Gentechnik abzulehnen. Der Mensch ist immer skeptisch, wenn es um etwas Neues geht. Wenn wir alle jede neue

Technik abgelehnt hätten, gäbe es heutzutage weder Autos noch Computer noch Handys!

N: Ich bin aktives Mitglied bei Greenpeace und arbeite im Moment an einer Flugblattkampagne gegen gentechnisch veränderte Lebensmittel. In meinen Augen stellen diese Lebensmittel ernsthafte Risiken dar. Es besteht die Gefahr, dass diese Produkte Allergien auslösen, da sie Eiweißstoffe beinhalten, die für den Menschen neu und ungewohnt sind. Was besonders kritisch ist, ist der Einsatz bestimmter antibiotischer Stoffe in Lebensmitteln. Das könnte zu Antibiotika-Resistenzen unter den Menschen führen und gefährliche Folgen haben. Ich glaube nicht, dass Gentechnik den Welthunger stillen könnte. Die meisten Entwicklungsländer und ihre Kleinbauern können sich die teure Technik überhaupt nicht leisten. Ich bin aber froh, dass jetzt härtere Regeln bestehen, um die Verbraucher zu schützen. EU-Regeln verlangen, dass alle Produkte, die auch nur die kleinste Menge an genmanipulierten Stoffen enthalten, gekennzeichnet werden müssen. Jetzt kann man gezielter einkaufen und diese Produkte vermeiden – man muss nur die Verpackung lesen.

3b Students listen to the opinions again and pick out the appropriate word from the box on the page to fill each gap. The box contains distractors.

Answers:

a *positive*
b *Entwicklungsländern*
c *Nährstoffe*
d *Milch*
e *Umweltorganisation*
f *Handzettel*
g *Allergien*
h *wirken*
i *skeptisch*
j *Verpackung*

4 A whole-class debate about the pros and cons of GM foods.

5 Students write 250 words about whether GM foods are the foodstuffs of the future. This could be done for homework.

Genforschung

Materials

- Students' Book pages 62–63
- CD 2, track 3

1 Use the cartoon to introduce the topic of cloning. Ask students (a) who the people in the cartoon are; (b) how they can choose the eye colour of their baby and (c) what they think of cloning.

2a Students read the text about genetic research.

2b Students create a spidergram on the topic of genetic research.

2c Students reread the text and decide whether the statements are true (R), false (F) or not mentioned in the text (N).

Answers:

a F **b** N **c** R **d** R **e** F **f** R **g** F **h** N
i R **j** R

2d Students translate the section of the text beginning *„Ein Embryo ist ein menschliches Lebewesen ... moralische Bedenken siegen wird.“* into English.

Answer:

'An embryo is a human living being, and so should not be experimented on. An embryo also has rights,' believes Gisela Wolf from the Aktion Leben group. 'Yes, I understand the advantages of the research, but the dangers pose too great a risk – how can we prevent unscrupulous solitary persons from cloning people? Ultimately, making money would win over any moral considerations.'

3 After listening to the report about gene technology, ask students to answer questions a–g in German to test comprehension.

Answers:

a *Erbkrankheiten / schon bei oder vor der Geburt / zu heilen*
b *Wissenschaftler entdeckten das Gen mit der betreffenden Mutation*
c *Menschliche Krankheiten werden im Labor imitiert, / damit gezielter nach neuen Wirkstoffen gesucht werden kann*
d *inwiefern ein Mensch die Veranlagung / für bestimmte Krankenheiten in sich trägt*
e *bei der Fortpflanzung*
f *sie wählte einen Embryo aus, /der die beste Chance hatte, passendes Knochenmark / für ihren krebskranken Sohn zu liefern*
g *Ein medizinischer Fortschritt / oder ein unethischer Eingriff in die Natur*

p 63, activity 3

Nirgendwo ist die Frage der Gentechnik umstrittener als in der Frage der Manipulation von menschlichen Organen. Durch diese Manipulation, so schätzen Wissenschaftler, wird es in der Zukunft möglich sein, Erbkrankheiten schon bei oder vor der Geburt zu heilen. Vor einigen Jahren entdecken Wissenschaftler das Gen mit der Mutation für zystische Fibrose. Man wartet noch auf einen Durchbruch, aber es ist keineswegs unrealistisch, dass diese Krankheit in der Zukunft heilbar sein wird. Die Gentherapie bietet auch Hoffnung für eine Reihe von Krankheiten wie Krebs und Aids. Im Bereich der Medizin bietet die Genforschung also viele Möglichkeiten. Menschliche Krankheiten werden im Labor imitiert, damit gezielter nach neuen Wirkstoffen gesucht werden kann. Auch kann abgeschätzt werden, inwiefern ein Mensch die Veranlagung für bestimmte Krankheiten in sich trägt. Wo soll das aber alles enden? Wollen wir gesundheitlich perfekte Menschen erzeugen? Wo liegen die ethischen Grenzen? Vor allem bei der Fortpflanzung ist das Thema umstritten. In Amerika ließ sich eine Frau künstlich befruchten, und wählte dann den Embryo aus, der die beste Chance hatte, passendes Knochenmark für ihren krebskranken Sohn zu liefern. Ein medizinischer Fortschritt oder ein unethischer Eingriff in die Natur, der die Einzigartigkeit des menschlichen Lebens in Frage stellt?

4 Students make notes on their own views on cloning in preparation for speaking to the whole class. They then have just one minute to express their views.

5 Students work in groups of four. Each student takes on one of the roles listed and the group has a debate on the topic of genetic research.

6 Students write a letter of about 250 words to an imaginary newspaper, setting out their views on cloning. This could be done for homework. Encourage them to draw upon the ideas presented on these pages of the Students' book for support.

Die Technikrevolution

Grammar focus

- The imperfect subjuntive

Materials

- Students' Book pages 64–65
- CD 2, track 4
- *Arbeitsblätter* 26, 28, 29
- Grammar Workbook page 59

1 A whole-class discussion about how the world will look in 20, 50 and 100 years' time. Incorporate the ideas from activity 1a on page 59.

2a The reading text deals with how technology is expected to change our lives. Students choose the appropriate sentence (1, 2 or 3) to end each sentence a–f.

Answers:
a 2 **b** 1 **c** 2 **d** 3 **e** 3 **f** 2

2b Ask students to list all the technical innovations mentioned in the text, along with any advantages and disadvantages they bring.

Answers:
Technische Fortschritte: *Brillen mit Internet-Zugang; Kreditkarte, auf der der vollständige Code des Inhabers gespeichert ist; Heimshopping; ein Internet der nächsten Generation; Videokonferenzen und Bildtelefone; elektronische Spracheingabe; automatische Übersetzungssysteme; Bauroboter*

Vorteile: *Heimshopping – man muss nicht in den Supermarkt gehen; elektronische Spracheingabe – einfache Schreibarbeiten werden entfallen; Videokonferenzen und Bildtelefone – Mitarbeiter werden nicht jeden Tag ins Büro fahren müssen*

Nachteile: *die Arbeitslosenquote wird sich erhöhen; Bauroboter werden Menschen ersetzen*

Grammatik

A Students practise forming the imperfect subjuntive from infinitives.

Answers:
a *wäre, könnte*
b *gingen*
c *käme*
d *müsste, hätten*

B Students now translate the sentences from A.

Answers:
a *If the Internet were/was faster, you could transmit moving pictures better.*
b *Because of teleworking, fewer people would go into the office.*
c *Because of the introduction of construction robots there would certainly be higher unemployment.*
d *So society would have to ensure that these people had the opportunity to get new jobs.*

C Students make up three sentences using the imperfect passive.

3 Students work in pairs to discuss which of the new technologies are worth having.

4 After listening to the text about robots, students answer questions a–g.

Answers:

a *Sie sind keine menschlichen Sportler, sondern Roboter.*
b *Kameras, Ultraschallsensoren und auf dem Rücken einen Laptop*
c *Sie erkennen ihre Umgebung, können Hindernisse umfahren und Elfmeter schießen.*
d *während des Spiels lernen*
e *zum Reinigen in Büros oder dafür, dass sie im Krankenhaus das Essen ausfahren*
f *Sie können selbstständig Aufgaben erledigen.*
g *Er führt Besucher durchs Deutsche Museum Bonn.*

p 65, activity 4

Int.: „Tor! Schon zum zweiten Mal in die linke Ecke", kommentierte der Besucher, der gebannt das Geschehen auf dem Spielfeld verfolgte. Hier ist aber kein normales Fußballspiel. Denn die Kicker sind keine menschlichen Sportler, sondern Roboter. Doktorand Steffen Gutmann erklärte:
S. G.: Sie haben Kameras, Ultraschallsensoren und auf dem Rücken einen Laptop. Mit all diesen Geräten erkennen sie ihre Umgebung, können Hindernisse umfahren und Elfmeter schießen. Nur während des Spiels lernen, das können die ‚Robocups' noch nicht. Lernen müssen sie offline. Wenn sie ausgeschaltet sind, werden Informationen eingegeben.
Int.: Außer dem Vergnügen – wozu sind solche Roboter gut? Man könnte sie zum Reinigen in Büros einsetzen oser dafür, dass sie im Krankenhaus das Essen ausfahren. Entscheidend ist, dass Roboter inzwischen so weit entwickelt sind, dass sie selbstständig Aufgaben erledigen können. Beispiele von solchen Robotern waren bei der Veranstaltung ‚Science fiction meets reality' zu sehen. Der größte Roboter, Rhino, kann Besucher durchs Deutsche Museum Bonn führen und das demnächst auch per Internet.

5 Ask students to list jobs in which people could be replaced with robots. Students' answers to activities 2b and 4 should help them.

6 Students work in pairs to answer the questions about the cartoon.

7 Students imagine that the MD of the company where they work wants to replace some members of staff with robots. They write him or her a letter giving their opinion about this. This could be done for homework.

A 26

Students listen to a report about the role of robots in landing on the planet Mars. They then do activity 1 on *Arbeitsblatt* 26

Prüfungstraining

Grammar and skills

- Using the future perfect
- Using the conditional perfect
- Improving your listening comprehension by completing gap-fill activities

Materials

- Students' Book pages 66–67
- CD 2, track 6
- *Arbeitsblatt* 30
- Grammar Workbook pages 61, 81

Grammatik

1 Students put these sentences into the future perfect.

Answers:

a *Forscher **werden** Heilmittel gegen schwere Krankheiten **gefunden haben**.*
b *Man **wird** gentechnisch verändertes Obst und Gemüse in der Wüste **angepflanzt haben**.*
c *Die Arbeitslosenquote **wird** durch die Technikrevolution **gestiegen sein**.*
d *Astronauten **werden** nach dem Mars **geflogen sein**.*
e *Man **wird** die Schule durch Lernen im Internet **ersetzt haben**.*
f *Wissenschaftler **werden** eine Impfung gegen Malaria **erfunden haben**.*

1b Students practise using the future perfect by writing sentences saying what they and their classmates will have done in ten years time.

Grammatik

2 Students complete the text with the correct form of the verb given in brackets in the conditional perfect.

Answers:
In Deutschland ist therapeutisches Klonen trotz Kampagnen mancher Politiker noch verboten. Wie

hätten *diese Jugendliche* ***gehandelt****, wenn sie* ***hätten bestimmen dürfen****, wie es mit dem therapeutischen Klonen in Deutschland weitergehen soll?*

Antonia: *Ich bin für therapeutisches Klonen und finde, dass die Politiker nicht genug getan haben, um unsere Aufmerksamkeit auf die Vorteile zu lenken. An ihrer Stelle* ***hätte*** *ich eine große Werbekampagne* ***geführt*** *und* ***hätte*** *auch Flugblätter* ***verteilt****, damit das Volk besser über die Vorteile informiert* ***gewesen wäre****.*

Hans*: Ich finde Klonen in allen Formen unmenschlich und* ***hätte*** *auf alle Fälle dagegen* ***gestimmt****. Ich* ***hätte*** *Bilder von kleinen Embryos* ***gezeigt****, damit man versteht, dass es hier um Menschen und nicht um Zellen geht. Ich* ***hätte*** *auch den potentiellen Missbrauch dieser Technik* ***betont****.*

3a Students listen to the report about an automated restaurant in Nuremberg.

p 67, activities 3a and 3b

In Nürnberg sorgt das neue Restaurant „'s Baggers" für Furore. Der Clou: Die Speisen gleiten auf Schienen zu den Tischen der Gäste – nur mit Hilfe der Schwerkraft. In kleinen Töpfen kommen Gerichte und Getränke direkt zum Tisch. Bestellt wird über einen Touchscreen. Ein Computersystem vernetzt das gesamte Restaurant. Während oben in der Küche die Wünsche der Gäste eingehen, errechnet das Programm die voraussichtliche Lieferzeit für Speisen und Getränke und gibt sie an die Gäste weiter. Kellner sind nirgendwo zu finden. Erfinder Michael Mack spricht von einer Revolution der Systemgastronomie: „Das Restaurant ohne Servicepersonal ist jetzt eine Tatsache." Speisen kommen schneller und wärmer zum Tisch. Und „'s Baggers" hat eine weitere Besonderheit – Bonussystem und bargeldloses Bezahlen mit Deutschlands erster Restaurant-Kundenkarte. Das moderne Restaurant kommt gut an: ohne Reservierung gibt es abends keine Plätze mehr, und weitere Filialien sind geplant.

Mit Automatisierung lassen sich Milliarden Euro an Personalkosten einsparen, und Dienstunternehmen sind zunehmend der Ansicht, sie können auf menschliche Arbeitskraft verzichten. An so genannten Hotelomaten können Reisende mit ihrer Kreditkarte 24 Stunden am Tag einchecken und einen Schlüssel erhalten. Empfangspersonal gibt es nicht mehr. Und in den Supermärkten ist es schon üblich, dass Kunden an manchen Kassen die Waren an Automaten selbst einscannen und bezahlen. Für Dienstunternehmen bedeutet es, dass sie Geld einsparen, und für die Kunden, dass sie schließlich weniger bezahlen, aber was passiert mit dem jetzt überflüssigen Personal?

3b Students listen again and complete the text with the words from the box.

Answers:

a *bedient*
b *aufgeben*
c *kommen*
d *geliefert*
e *auskommt*
f *gebraucht*
g *reservieren*
h *anbieten*
i *begrüßt*
j *kassieren*
k *reduzieren*
l *steigt*

Zur Auswahl

Skills focus

- Revision of unit

Materials

- Students' Book page 68
- Solo CD , track 7

S 

1 Students listen to the report and complete the text.

Answers:

a *Umzug*
b *Geräten*
c *Luft*
d *Verbrauch*
e *Bezahlung*
f *Rechnungen*
g *Nachrichten*
h *Unterstützung*
i *Aufträge*
j *Stimme*
k *Entwicklung*
l *Hinweise*

p 68, activity 1

Mi Yung Kim und ihr kleiner Sohn Jae Won sind vor zwei Monaten in ihre neue Wohnung eingezogen. Auf den ersten Blick sieht sie wie jede andere Wohnung aus – aber diese neuen Wohnungen in Seoul, Korea, sind alle mit den neuesten technischen Geräten ausgestattet. Alles in der Wohnung wird von einem integrierten Computersystem über ein Heimnetz gesteuert. Das Netz kontrolliert die Klimaanlage, gibt Auskunft über

den Stromverbrauch, zahlt automatisch Rechnungen und nimmt Videonachrichten auf. Der Fernseher ist ebenfalls mit integriert, und so sieht Mi Yung eine Nachricht auf dem Bildschirm, wenn die Waschmaschine sich ausschaltet oder wenn jemand an der Tür klingelt.
Alle Daten werden gespeichert und sind über das Internet zugänglich. Wenn Mi Yung nicht zu Hause ist, kann sie problemlos herausfinden, wer vorbeigeschaut oder wer eine Nachricht hinterlassen hat. Die Elektronikfirma LG steckt hinter diesen Zukunftswohnungen, die in den nächsten fünf Jahren für weitere 30 000 Koreaner Alltag werden sollen. Und dabei wird es nicht bleiben – in der nächsten Version sollen alle Geräte in der Wohnung nicht nur stimmgesteuert, sondern auch hilfsbereit sein, beispielswiese ein Kühlschrank, der Rezepttipps gibt und vor verfaultem Gemüse warnt.

2a Students read the text about the Tasmanian Tiger.

2b Students answer the questions in German to ensure they have understood the text.

Answers:

a *Die Wissenschaftler haben eine DNA-Probe des bereits Ende der 30er Jahre ausgestorbenen Tasmanischen Tigers isoliert, in Mäuseembryos verpflanzt und ihn so zum Leben erweckt.*
b *Die Wissenschaftler werden neue Verfahren und praktische Anwendungsmöglichkeiten für die Biologie und die Medizin entwickeln können.*
c *Man könnte theoretisch den Tasmanischen Tiger klonen.*
d *Andere Wissenschafter sind skeptisch über das Klonen ausgestorbener Tiere, weil man nicht in der Welt des Jurassic Park lebt.*

2c Students discuss the questions listed with a partner.

3 Students write a 200-word report on one of the following topics: cloning, GM foods, or renewable energy sources.

4 Students translate sentences a–f , practising some of the vocabulary from the unit.

Answers:

a *Lebensmittel können durch Gentechnik verändert werden.*
b *Alle gemanipulierten Lebensmittel müssen gekennzeichnet werden.*
c *Die Vorteile von Gentechnik sind umstritten.*
d *Technische Fortschritte werden den Arbeitsplatz revolutionieren.*
e *Es ist möglich, dass Roboter Menschen ersetzen werden.*
f *Alternative Methoden der Energiegewinnung müssen entwickelt werden, um den Energiebedarf der Welt zu decken.*

Wiederholung Einheit 5–6

Materials

- Students' Book, pages 69–70
- CD 2, track 7

1a Students read the text about the role of the press.

1b Students read the text again and then find the appropriate sentence for each of a–d.

Answers:
a 3 **b** 3 **c** 1 **d** 2

1c To further test their comprehension, students answer the questions on the text.

Answers:

a *Obwohl sie die Namen geändert hatte, wusste man wer gemeint war, weil es in einer kleinen Stadt passiert war; das Mädchen musste die schrecklichen Ereignisse noch einmal durchleben.*
b *Weil die Reporterin viel Geld verdienen wollte und mehr Zeitungen verkauft werden.*
c *Weil sie auch Verständnis für die Großmutter hatte.*
d *Sie versucht auch für die Situation der Großmutter Verständnis zu wecken.*
e *Sie liebt ihren Beruf, aber manchmal ist es schwer, wenn man über etwas Unangenehmes schreiben muss.*

2 Students read the opinions in the speech bubbles. Which views do they agree with? They should come up with further arguments which back up their point of view. They then defend their point of view against a partner with an opposing view.

3a Students listen to the report.

p 70, activities 3a and 3b

Wussten Sie, dass Sie sich schon jetzt für eine Reise zum Mars anmelden können? Im Jahr 2018 sollen Astronauten zum Mond zurückkehren, und ab 2030 sollen Touristen dann nicht nur den Mond, sondern auch den roten Planeten in komfortablen

Weltraumfähren erreichen können. Reisedauer zum Mars: 100 Tage – da muss natürlich dafür gesorgt werden, dass die Weltraumtouristen bequem reisen. Ein Münchner Architekt hat mit den Studenten der TU München Weltraummöbel entworfen, so zum Beispiel ein Weltraumbett. Wegen der Schwerelosigkeit in einer Raumfähre muss man sich an das Bett festbinden, denn sonst wacht man am nächsten Morgen ganz woanders auf. Wie Astronauten dem Architekten und seinen Studenten mitteilten, vermissen sie den Druck der Bettdecke. Daraufhin hat er aufblasbare Halterungen entworfen, die dieses Gefühl erzeugen sollen.

Außerdem werden auch Raumstationen gebaut werden müssen. Zur Zeit ist jedoch die Frage des Standorts ein Problem. Wo genau soll die Mondstation hin? Die ideale Lösung wäre eine mobile Mondstation. Die Kosten für ein solches Projekt werden zwischen 40 und 50 Milliarden Dollar betragen, also muss man den Standort genau planen. Bei der Planung für Mars wird man die gleichen Fragen stellen müssen: bewegliche oder unterirdische Stationen? Denn man darf nicht vergessen, dass auf dem Mars die ultraviolette Strahlung sehr hoch ist und es außerdem Windgeschwindigkeiten bis zu 360 Stundenkilometern geben kann.

[from: Architektur fürs All, in Das 3sat-Fernsehmagazin, Ausgabe 2/ 2006, p.4]

3b A true/false activity to test comprehension. Students decide which of the statements are true (R), false (F) or not in the text (N).

Answers:
a R **b** F **c** N **d** F **e** F **f** N **g** R **h** F

4 Students translate the passage into English.

Answer:
Part of the 'good living' project in space includes a Dutch architect's plans. His 'Lunatic' hotel is in the form of 160-metre high towers. Such a construction is, of course, only possible because no wind blows on the Moon, and the force of gravity is much lower than it is on the Earth. The hotel rooms should be hanging freely from the construction, and in order to ent
ertain the guests, they will be offered bat wings for flying.

5 Students answer the questions orally. Encourage them to use the ideas and vocabulary covered in Unit 6.

6 Students write an essay saying to what extent they agree with the statement that our society is responsible for the high crime rates amongst young people. They should mention the points listed and should draw upon the ideas and vocabulary presented on these pages of the Student's Book for support.

Literatur, Film und die bildende Kunst Einheit 7

Unit objectives

By the end of this unit students will be able to:

- Discuss what makes a good read
- Describe their favourite book and discuss their favourite author
- Discuss the main characters and the plot of a German film of their choice
- Express an opinion about the work of a painter or a musician of their choice
- Discuss and compare musicians from German-speaking countries
- Discuss the importance of literature and the arts in today's society

Grammar

By the end of this unit students will be able to:

- Use the subjunctive in other ways

Skills

By the end of this unit students will be able to:

- Plan and develop ideas for an essay

Materials

- Students' Book page 71

1 Students match the descriptions to the pictures.

Answers:

a *Jazz ist anders (4)*
b *Crazy (6)*
c *Kirschblüten (8)*
d *Die Vermessung der Welt (1)*
e *Klimt (3)*
f *Goodbye Lenin (7)*
g *Der Vorleser (2)*
h *Von Herzen – Das Beste (5)*

Die Lust am Lesen

Materials

- Students' Book pages 72–73
- CD 2, tracks 8–9

1 Students listen to the recording and fill in the table.

Answers:

Johann Wolfgang von Goethe – Dichter – Die Leiden des jungen Werther, Faust

Friedrich Dürrenmatt – Dramatiker – Der Richter und sein Henker, Die Physiker

Heinrich Böll – Romanschriftsteller – Die verlorene Ehre der Katharina Blum, Gruppenbild mit Dame

Günther Grass – Romanschriftsteller – Die Blechtrommel

Bertolt Brecht – Dramatiker – Dreigroschenoper, Mutter Courage

p 72, activity 1

Erster Jugendlicher:	Was lest ihr denn so im Deutschunterricht? Wir haben gerade ‚Die Leiden des jungen Werther' gelesen. Ich fand das ein tolles Buch und immer noch echt aktuell, obwohl es im Jahr 1774 geschrieben wurde. Dieser Typ, der junge Werther, ist ziemlich cool und hat ähnliche Probleme wie wir Jugendliche heute.
Zweite Jugendliche:	Ehrlich? Wer hat das Buch denn geschrieben?
Erster Jugendlicher:	Das weißt du nicht? Mann, das ist aber 'ne Bildungslücke! Der alte Goethe natürlich, **der** Dichter überhaupt. Johann Wolfgang von Goethe…
Zweite Jugendliche:	Ach so, ja, von Goethe haben wir den ‚Faust' gelesen und dann die Filmversion gesehen. Aber das war mir etwas zu heavy. Zur Zeit lesen wir ‚Der Richter und sein Henker'…
Dritter Jugendlicher:	Das ist doch von Friedrich Dürrenmatt, einem Schweizer Dramatiker, oder? Der hat auch das Theaterstück ‚Die Physiker' geschrieben. Es geht darin um drei Physiker in einer Irrenanstalt.

Zweite Jugendliche:	Das Stück kenne ich nicht, aber ‚Der Richter und sein Henker' ist ein interessanter Krimi. Es geht darin um das perfekte Verbrechen. Und danach lesen wir mal etwas Moderneres und zwar den Roman ‚Die verlorene Ehre der Katharina Blum' von Heinrich Böll.
Dritter Jugendlicher:	Das ist ein ziemlich politisches Buch, nicht? Geht es nicht um die Sensationspresse und das Thema Terrorismus in Deutschland in den 70er Jahren? Wir haben den Roman ‚Gruppenbild mit Dame' von Böll gelesen; der spielt in den 30er und 40er Jahren, und ich fand ihn wirklich gut. Ich interessiere mich für geschichtliche Themen und würde gern den Roman ‚Die Blechtrommel' von Günther Grass lesen. Darin geht es um das Leben Oskars in der Zeit zwischen den beiden Weltkriegen.
Erster Jugendlicher:	Wie findet ihr denn Bertolt Brecht? Der hat doch die‚Dreigroschenoper' geschrieben, und sein bekanntestes Theaterstück ist, glaube ich, ‚Mutter Courage'. Ich habe die englische Version im Fernsehen gesehen.
Zweite Jugendliche:	Die ‚Dreigroschenoper' gefällt mir besser, weil ich die Musik von Kurt Weill toll finde, besonders ‚Die Moritat von Mackie Messer'.

2a Students read the text about Julia Franck and Katharina Hacker.

2b Students read the statements and choose the correct answer.

Answers:

a 3 **b** 2 **c** 2 **d** 3

2c Students now answer the questions in German.

Answers:

a *Er wurde mit dem Deutschen Buchpreis 2007 ausgezeichnet, er ist seit Oktober 2007 ein Bestseller, und man hat schon 350 000 Exemplare verkauft.*

b *Eine Rückblende beschreibt Ereignisse, die in der Vergangenheit der Protagonisten stattgefunden haben und helfen sollen, die Gegenwart besser zu verstehen.*

c *Students express their own opinion.*

d *Der Roman spielt zur Zeit der Anschläge auf das World Trade Center 2001, sowie des Irak-Kriegs im März 2003.*

e *Students express their own opinion: for example, Die Protagonisten sind trotz ihres Erfolges nicht glücklich; sie wissen viel, aber sie kennen sich nicht selbst. Sie fragen nicht nach dem Sinn ihres Lebens/Sie haben materielle Güter, aber sonst nichts.*

3 Students listen to an interview, read the statements and decide if they are true (R), false (F) or not mentioned (N).

Answers:

a F **b** F **c** F **d** R **e** N **f** R **g** R **h** N **i** F

p 73, activity 3

Interviewer
Wir machen hier ein Interview zum Thema „Was die heutigen Jugendlichen so in ihrer Freizeit lesen". Heike, vielen Dank, dass Sie mitmachen.

Heike
Ich lese gern Bücher von Bernhard Schlink. Das erste Buch, das ich von ihm gelesen habe, war der Krimi ‚Selbstjustiz'. Was mir besonders gefallen hat, war die raffinierte und sarkastische Handlung des Krimis. Das zweite Buch war kein Krimi, aber trotzdem unheimlich interessant. Ich hätte das ganze Buch am liebsten auf einmal gelesen. Der Roman heißt ‚Der Vorleser', und es geht darin um einen 15-jährigen Jungen – Michael Berg –, der eine 20 Jahre ältere Frau, Hanna Schmitz, kennen lernt. Sie ist Straßenbahnschaffnerin und hilft ihm, als ihm eines Tages in der Straßenbahn schlecht wird. Als es ihm wieder besser geht, besucht er sie, weil er sich bei ihr bedanken möchte. Langsam entwickelt sich eine Liebesbeziehung zwischen dem ungleichen Paar mit einem besonderen Ritual. Jedesmal, bevor sie sich lieben, muss Michael Hanna vorlesen. Eines Tages verschwindet Hanna plötzlich. Jahre später sieht er sie wieder, als sie mit anderen ehemaligen KZ-Aufseherinnen unter Anklage steht. Michael erkennt nun, warum er ihr immer vorlesen musste: Sie ist Analphabetin,

schämte sich aber, es ihm zu sagen. Sie wird zu lebenslanger Haft verurteilt, und Michael, der sich an dem Urteil mitschuldig fühlt, nimmt im Gefängnis wieder Kontakt zu ihr auf. Die Geschichte nimmt ein unerwartetes Ende, aber das liest man am besten selbst. Es ist wirklich ein fantastischer Roman und ein Weltbestseller, der in 27 Sprachen übersetzt und mit mehreren Preisen ausgezeichnet wurde.

4 Students work with a partner to discuss their favourite book.

5 Students choose one of the authors mentioned in the reading or writing text and write a passage summarising his/her life and work. They should also give reasons for choosing this author. Encourage them to read the *Tipp* section on page 79 for support.

Geheimtipp: Der neue deutsche Film

Materials

- Students' Book pages 74–75
- CD 2, track 10

1 Students discuss the questions listed either as a class or in pairs.

2a Students read the information about German film from the 70s to today.

2b Students explain what each of the expressions from the text means.

Answers:

a *Die Sensationspresse kann durch ungenaue, verzerrte oder unwahre Berichte/Artikel das Leben von unschuldigen Menschen zerstören.*
b *Eine Gesellschaft hat so viele Vorurteile und so viele Regeln und Erwartungen, dass man sich nicht mehr frei fühlt.*
c *Es gibt weniger Besucher.*
d *lustige Filme, in denen es um menschliche Beziehungen geht*
e *ein finanzieller Erfolg für Kinos/sie verkaufen viele Kinokarten*

2c Students read through the text again and complete the sentences.

Answers:

a *...Terrorismus und die Auswirkungen der Sensationspresse auf das Leben unschuldiger Menschen dargestellt.*
b *...unglückliche Liebesbeziehungen in einer repressiven Gesellschaft mit Vorurteilen.*
c *...die Leute nicht mehr ins Kino gingen und so viele Kinos schließen mussten.*
d *...Beziehungskomödien und satirische Komödien besonders beliebt.*
e *...wieder mehr Anerkennung, guten Kritiken und Nominierungen für Filmpreise.*

3a Students match the German and English expressions.

Answers:

a 2 **b** 4 **c** 6 **d** 5 **e** 1 **f** 3

3b Students listen to a telephone conversation between two young people discussing a film.

p 75, activities 3b, 3c and 3d

Franjo: Hallo?
Lisa: Hallo, Franjo, hier ist Lisa. Na, wie war's gestern Abend im Kino? Was habt ihr gesehen?
Franjo: Ach, du, es war so schade, dass du nicht mit uns kommen konntest. Wir haben den Film ‚Good Bye, Lenin' gesehen, und ich fand ihn einfach sagenhaft.
Lisa: Oooch, Mensch, das ist doch der Film von Wolfgang Becker, der den Deutschen Filmpreis für die beste Regie bekam, und Daniel Brühl wurde als bester Hauptdarsteller ausgezeichnet, richtig?
Franjo: Ja, genau. Und ich muss sagen, Daniel Brühl war total gut – der ist einfach so natürlich und irgendwie so unschuldig, ohne naiv zu sein. In seiner Rolle als Alex ist er einfach so sympatisch. Er tut alles nur Mögliche, um seine Mutter ja nicht aufzuregen und...
Lisa: Bevor du weiter machst, worum geht es eigentlich genau? Ich weiß nur, dass die Handlung zur Zeit der Wende spielt.
Franjo: Das stimmt, aber der Film beginnt in den 70er Jahren, als sich Alex' Vater in den Westen absetzt. Christiane, seine Frau und die Kinder Alex und Ariane sollen später nachkommen. Aber aus Angst bleibt Christiane mit den Kindern im Osten und beginnt nach anfänglicher Skepsis, sich für den Sozialismus zu engagieren. Zum 40. Jahrestag der DDR soll sie eine Auszeichnung bekommen, aber auf dem Weg dorthin sieht sie, wie ihr Sohn Alex bei einer Demonstration von der Volkspolizei geschlagen und festgenommen wird. Sie hat einen Zusammenbruch und wird ins

Krankenhaus gebracht, wo sie im Koma liegt. Vom Fall der Mauer bekommt sie nichts mit und auch nichts von den folgenden Veränderungen. Alex arbeitet als Vertreter für Satelittenschüsseln und seine Schwester bei Burger King. Sie verliebt sich in einen Westdeutschen, Alex in die russische Krankenschwester Lara. Als seine Mutter schließlich aus dem Koma aufwacht, darf sie sich nicht aufregen, sonst könnte es fatale Folgen haben. Da sie von den Veränderungen der letzten Monate nichts weiß und nichts wissen darf, will Alex die ‚alte' DDR in ihrer Wohnung wieder aufleben lassen. Das bringt natürlich eine Menge Probleme mit sich und hat viele total witzige Szenen mit Anspielungen auf das Leben in der ehemaligen DDR. Schließlich erfährt die Mutter die Wahrheit von Lara, und sie ist so beeindruckt und gerührt von Alex' Bemühungen, dass sie Alex im Glauben lässt, sie wisse nichts. Als sie drei Tage vor dem ersten Jahrestag der deutschen Einheit stirbt, glaubt Alex, dass sie glücklich starb, im Glauben, dass die DDR dem Westen überlegen sei.

Lisa: Das hört sich ja wirklich gut an…

Franjo: Ist es auch, was ich besonders toll finde, ist, wie der Film auf liebenswerte, wenn auch leicht ironische Art die Eigentümlichkeiten der DDR aufzeigt und die damaligen politischen Ereignisse widerspiegelt. Und weil es eine Komödie ist, gibt es trotz des ernsten Themas viele witzige Anspielungen. Ich würde dir empfehlen, den Film unbedingt anzuschauen.

3c To test their comprehension the conversation, students read the statements and find the five that are false.

Answers:

a R **b** F **c** F **d** R **e** R **f** R **g** F **h** R **i** F **j** R **k** F

3d Students listen again and make notes on the points listed.

4 Students choose their favourite film and describe it to the class, using the points listed as prompts, but without mentioning the name of the film or the name of the lead. The class tries to guess what the film is.

5 Students choose one of the films mentioned on page 74. They try to find out as much as possible about the director and the lead. They then write 200-250 words recording their findings. Encourage them to draw upon the vocabulary presented on these pages of the Students' Book for support.

Musik und Malerei

Materials

- Students' Book pages 76–77
- CD 2, track 11
- *Arbeitsblätter* 31, 32

1a Students study the three pictures and decide which they associate with German music and why. They then discuss this as a class.

1b Students discuss any other German-speaking musicians or bands that they know of.

1c Students look at the pictures. As a class, they then discuss the artists featured and their work and any other German-speaking artists they know of.

2a Students read the text about the German group, *Tokio Hotel.*

2b Students answer the questions on the text to test their comprehension.

Answers:

a *Sie sind auch im Ausland bekannt und beliebt.*

b *In den USA, weil die Konzerte ausverkauft waren und man Karten nur noch auf dem Schwarzmarkt kaufen konnte/Ein Fan wollte deutsch lernen.*

c *Israelische Fans haben 5000 Unterschriften gesammelt.*

d *Musikproduzent Peter Hoffmann entdeckte die Band, und die Universal Music Group bot ihnen einen Vertrag an.*

e *Sie sind noch etwas jung/unreif für die Texte, die sie schreiben.*

2c Students translate the sentences into German.

Answers:

a *Einige Eintrittskarten waren auf dem Schwarzmarkt verkauft worden, nachdem man an der Kasse keine Karten mehr kaufen konnte.*

b *Wenn die Fans in Israel nicht so viele Unterschriften gesammelt hätten, hätte die Band nicht in Tel Aviv gespielt.*

c *Ihre eigene Zeitschrift zu produzieren war Teil des Marketingplans, den die Universal Music Group der Band angeboten hatte.*

2d Students translate the last section into English.

Answer:
As far as Tokio Hotel's *music, lyrics and videos are concerned, they could be described as a rock group. The four members of the group are still very young. Although when they were discovered in 2003 they were regarded as a 'Boyband', their lyrics deal with subjects that you would more likely attribute to more mature musicians. But it is exactly this contrast that makes the group so loved by their fans.*

3a Students read the text about the Austrian painter, Gustav Klimt.

3b They then choose the most appropriate ending for a–d.

Answers:
a 3 **b** 1 **c** 3 **d** 2

4a Students listen to two young people discussing German groups.

p 77, activities 4a, 4b and 4c

Katja: Sag mal, Ben, was findest du denn so toll an Rammstein?
Ben: Also, alle sechs Bandmitglieder, sie kommen übrigens aus Ostdeutschland, sind wirklich gute Musiker. Die spielen einfach einen tollen Hardrock. Außerdem singen sie auf Deutsch – da kann man wenigstens verstehen, was sie singen. Ihre Texte finde ich auch cool, weil sie ziemlich provokativ sind.
Katja: OK, aber die sind doch bestimmt nur in Deutschland bekannt, wenn sie nur deutschsprachige Songs, ooops – ich meine natürlich Lieder – singen?
Ben: Nein, im Gegenteil. In den USA zum Beispiel hat die Band schon über eine Million CDs verkauft. Und 1999 wurden sie für den Musikpreis ‚Grammy' nominiert. ‚Rammstein' hat auch viele Tourneen durch die USA gemacht, und ihre Konzerte sind total ausverkauft. Aber deutscher Hardrock ist auch in Australien, Skandinavien und Osteuropa gefragt.
Katja: Kannst du mir mal was von ‚Rammstein' vorspielen?
Ben: Na klar, aber du kannst dir auch den amerikanischen Film ‚Triple X' anschauen, da kannst du sie sehen und hören, aber warte, ich spiel dir [title of song] vor.
Katja: Na ja, wenn man Hardrock mag, sind sie nicht schlecht. Was hältst du denn von der Gruppe ‚Wise Guys'? Ich weiß, die Musik ist total anders, aber …
Ben: Ich hab schon irgendwann mal von der Band gehört, der Name ist mir bekannt, aber was für Musik machen die genau?
Katja: Sie sind eine A-capella-Gruppe – das heißt, es gibt keine Instrumente und sie machen alle musikalischen Geräusche selber. Sie komponieren alle Lieder selbst. Ich finde ihre Texte einfach sagenhaft, weil sie intelligent und oft witzig oder ironisch sind. Als A-capella-Gruppe sind ihre Lieder natürlich alle sehr rhythmisch. In Deutschland wurden die ‚Wise Guys' 2001 mit dem Lied und dem Videoclip ‚Jetzt ist Sommer' bekannt. Aber im Gegensatz zu ‚Rammstein' geben die ‚Wise Guys' überwiegend in deutschsprachigen Ländern Konzerte, obwohl sie 2006 auch in London auftraten. Ich spiel mal ‚Jetzt ist Sommer', in Ordnung?

4b Students fill in the gaps. Remind them to check that their answers are grammatically correct.

Answers:
a *sechs*
b *dem*
c *Deutsch*
d *Ausland*
e *ausverkauften*
f *ohne*
g *bekannteste*
h *2001*
i *intelligente*
j *witzige/ironischen*

4c Students listen to the recording again and note down differences between the two groups.

5 Students choose a German-speaking group, musician or painter and write a description of him/her (200–250 words) including what they especially like about his/her work and why they have chosen this person.

Prüfungstraining

Grammar and skills

- Using the subjunctive in other ways
- Research skills

Materials

- Students' Book pages 78–79
- Grammar Workbook pages 59, 82–83
- *Arbeitsblätter* 34 and 35

1 Students translate the sentences into German. Refer them back to part A of the *Grammatik* section for support.

Answers:
- **a** *Wenn wir ins Kino gegangen wären, hätten wir Johnny Depp getroffen.*
- **b** *Wenn du den neuen Roman von Daniel Kehlmann gekauft hättest, hättest du seine Unterschrift/sein Autogramm bekommen.*
- **c** *Wenn sein Computer nicht kaputt gewesen wäre, hätte er mehr Informationen gefunden.*
- **d** *Das Konzert hätte nicht stattgefunden, wenn niemand gekommen wäre.*

2 Students fill in the correct form of the verb. Refer them back to part B of the *Grammatik* section for support.

Answers:
- **a** *warnen müssen*
- **b** *gemusst*
- **c** *sehen lassen dürfen*
- **d** *lesen sollen*

3 Students rewrite the sentences as polite requests. Refer them back to part C of the *Grammatik* section for support.

Answers:
- **a** *Es wäre nett, wenn Sie die Tür zumachten.*
- **b** *Ich hätte gern eine neue DVD.*
- **c** *Sie möchte gern ein größeres Zimmer.*
- **d** *Ich wäre dir dankbar, wenn du mir bitte beim Kochen helfen würdest.*
- **e** *Wir möchten den Krimi gern jetzt sehen.*

4 Students complete the sentences. Refer them back to part D of the *Grammatik* section for support.

Answers:
- **a** *Bauchweh habe*
- **b** *kennten wir sie nicht*
- **c** *hätten sie Hunger (using the imperfect subjunctive here as the present subjunctive is the same as the indicative)*
- **d** *gewesen wäre*
- **e** *verstanden hätte*

5 Students research the work of either a painter or an architect from a German-speaking country and prepare for the essay title by following the *Tipp* step by step.

6 Students research the work of a writer from a German-speaking country and prepare for the essay by following the *Tipp* step by step.

Zur Auswahl

Materials
- Students' Book page 80
- Solo CD, track 8
- *Arbeitsblatt* 33

1a Students study the cartoons and answer the questions orally.

1b Students discuss their point of view with a partner or as a class.

2a Students read the text about Mies van der Rohe.

2b Students translate the second section into English.

Answer:
He also built housing estates, like the Weißenhofsiedlung in Stuttgart which represents the project 'new building'. In 1930 he is appointed by Walter Gropius as director of Bauhaus, the famous art, design and architectural school. The Bauhaus school, however, had to be closed in 1933, as the Nazis were ill-disposed towards the idea of this modern architecture. As it was no longer possible for Mies van der Rohe to work as an architect under the Nazi regime, he emigrated to the USA in 1938. There, he built amongst others the tower blocks at Lake Shore Drive in Chicago, as well as the Chicago Federal Center. Four years before his death, he is commissioned to build the new National Gallery in Berlin. He died in Chicago in 1969.

2c Students find out about one of the two other architects mentioned and write a short summary about him.

3a Students listen to a report about a famous German Jazz trumpeter.

> p 80, activities 3a and 3b
>
> Er gab schon Konzerte mit Dave Brubeck, Chaka Khan, Natalie Cole, Tony Bennett und Klaus Doldinger, um nur einige Jazz-größen zu nennen.

> Seine erste eigene CD hieß ‚Generations of Jazz', und er erhielt dafür den Preis der Deutschen Plattenindustrie und den Preis der Deutschen Schallplattenkritik. 1998 erschien sein Debütalbum ‚Love'. Er war sowohl Komponist als auch Arrangeur und Produzent von verschiedenen Soloalben anderer Sänger. Im Jahr 2002 machte er eine Tournee in Thailand und Japan, und seit 2004 präsentiert er seine eigene Show ‚Talkin' Jazz', zu der er einen prominenten Gast einlädt, mit dem er sich über Jazz unterhält. Seine DVD ‚A Night in Berlin', die 2005 erschien, bekam den ‚DVD Champion Award 2005'. Seine Musik, einschließlich seiner neuesten CD ‚Oceana', ist vor allem bei Frauen beliebt, die von seinem eleganten Trompetenklängen begeistert sind. Sie haben sicher erraten, um wen es sich hier handelt? Natürlich – es ist Till Brönner!

S 

3b Students complete the sentences.

Answers:

a *...Jazzgrößen/berühmten Musikern Konzerte gegeben.*
b *...Komponist, Arrangeur und Produzent.*
c *...er sich über Jazz in seiner eigenen Show ‚Talkin' Jazz'.*
d *...die DVD ‚A Night in Berlin'.*
e *...seine neueste CD/seine eleganten Trompetenklänge.*

4 Students write an essay on one of the topics listed. They should write at least 250 words and should use the *Tipp* on page 79 for support.

Deutschland heute Einheit 8

Unit objectives

By the end of this unit students will be able to:

- Discuss the building and fall of the Berlin wall
- Discuss life in the new, reunited Germany
- Discuss the role of Germany in the EU
- Talk about some typical German festivals

Grammar

By the end of this unit students will be able to:

- Use the passive

Skills

By the end of this unit students will be able to:

- Answer questions in German

Materials

- Students' Book page 81

1 Students work in pairs and select two of the bullet points to write about. They can use the earlier chapters of the book to look things up. Students then share their notes with the class.

Berlin – die geteilte Stadt

Grammar focus

- The passive

Materials

- Students' Book pages 82–83
- CD 2, tracks 12–13
- Grammar Workbook page 64

1a Students read the report by Johann Segers and his son, Karl about the building and fall of the Berlin wall.

1b Students fill in the gaps with the appropriate word from the box.

Answers:

a *Bau*
b *Flucht*
c *Absperrung*
d *Transportsystem*
e *Erlaubnis*
f *Überwachung*
g *Kindheit*
h *Gewalt*
i *Erlaubnis, Überraschung*
j *Wendepunkt, Entschluss*

2 Students listen to the account of the events leading up to the fall of the Berlin wall and then match the dates to the events.

Answers:

a 4 **b** 6 **c** 1 **d** 2 **e** 8 **f** 9 **g** 3 **h** 7 **i** 5

p 83, activity 2

Historikerin

Wie ist es also zum Fall der Mauer gekommen? Innerhalb von ein paar Monaten ging ein System, das die Deutschen 40 Jahre lang geteilt hatte, zugrunde. Mehrere Faktoren spielten eine Rolle, sowohl der Mut der Ostdeutschen als auch der Unwille der Sowjets, wieder mit Panzern auf die Straße zu gehen. Die Geschichte beginnt mit einer Flüchtlingswelle. Im August begannen die DDR-Bürger ihr Land über andere Ostblockstaaten zu verlassen. Am 19. August konnten 600 Ostdeutsche über Ungarn nach Österreich kommen, am 10. September gewährte der ungarische Außenminister weiteren DDR-Flüchtlingen die Ausreise in die Bundesrepublik. Immer mehr Flüchtlinge wagten jetzt die Reise in den Westen. Am 30. September durften Flüchtlinge aus Prag und Warschau reisen, insgesamt 22 000 Flüchtlinge sind in der ersten Oktoberwoche auf diesem Weg in die Bundesrepublik gekommen. Trotz der wachsenden Krise ließ der SED-Chef den 40. Jahrestag der DDR am 7. Oktober feiern. Die Feier entwickelte sich aber teilweise zu Krawallen, als die Polizei Demonstrierende niederschlug. Zwei Tage später demonstrierten 70 000 Menschen in Leipzig. „Wir sind das Volk", riefen sie. Ein Volk hatte seine Angst verloren. Anfang November hob die tschechische Regierung die Visumspflicht für DDR-Bürger auf. Hier war also ein freier Weg in den Westen, den 50 000 DDR-Bürger in den nächsten Tagen benutzten. Drei Tage später demonstrierten etwa eine Million Menschen in Berlin. Die Regierung war ratlos. Am 8. November trat sie zurück und einen Tag darauf verkündete Josef Schabowski: „Um befreundete Staaten zu entlasten, hat man sich entschlossen, die Grenzübergänge zu öffnen. Wenn ich richtig informiert bin, gilt diese Regelung unmittelbar." Die Grenze war offen.

3 Students role-play a journalist interviewing someone who was in Berlin on 9 November 1989. The bullet points will help the journalist to ask appropriate questions.

4 Students imagine they were in Berlin when the wall came down and they write a newspaper article describing the events leading up to the famous day. This could be done for homework.

5 Students listen to the account of the day of German unity and answer the questions.

Answers:

a *Es war der Tag, an dem Deutschland wieder vereint wurde.*
b *Mit Feuerwerk, Böllerschüssen und einem ökumenischen Gottesdienst.*
c *Bundeskanzler und Bundespräsident*
d *friedliche Partnerschaft*
e *Mit Freibier und Feuerwerk*
f *Sie hat ihre Rolle als Hauptstadt verloren.*

p 83 activity 5

Um Mitternacht am 3. Oktober 1990 begann eine neue Epoche der deutschen Geschichte. In Berlin feierten Hunderttausende am Reichstag und am Brandenburger Tor, als um null Uhr die Bundesfahne als Zeichen der Einheit gehisst wurde. Das Fest wurde dann mit Feuerwerk und Böllerschüssen fortgesetzt. Die offiziele Feier ging mit einem ökumenischen Gottesdienst in der Berliner Marienkirche weiter. Im anschließenden Staatsakt versprach Bundeskanzler Kohl den Völkern der Welt friedliche Partnerschaft. Bundespräsident von Weizsäcker sagte: „Sich zu vereinen, heißt teilen lernen." Auch in anderen Städten wurde gefeiert. In Bonn, das bald seine Rolle als Hauptstadt verlieren würde, wurde Freibier ausgegeben, in Hamburg erlebten 500 000 ein Feuerwerk.

Grammatik

A Students change the sentences into the passive.

Answers:

a *Den DDR-Bürgern wurden nur selten erlaubt, Westberlin zu besuchen.*
b *In Leipzig ist gegen die DDR-Regierung demonstriert worden.*
c *Die Mauer wurde zerstört.*

B Students find all the examples expressing the passive in the texts on page 82 and translate them into English.

Deutschland seit der Wende

Materials

- Students' Book pages 84–85
- CD 2, tracks 14–15

1 Students start thinking about the differences between the former West and East Germany by dividing the bullet points between the headings.

Answers:

BRD: *moderne Technik, freie Marktwirtschaft, Demokratie*

DDR: *keine Bananen, Haushaltstage für arbeitende Mütter, altmodische Autos und Elektrogeräte, keine Arbeitslosigkeit, kostenlose Sozialeinrichtungen wie Kindergärten, Reisefreiheit nur in andere Ostblockstaaten*

2 Students listen to Thomas' account of life since the fall of the Berlin wall and then answer the questions.

Answers:

a *Demokratie, Reisefreiheit, Produkte zum Kauf.*
b *Sie haben den Leuten nachspioniert, um sich zu vergewissern, dass man nichts unternommen hatte, was gegen den kommunistischen Staat war.*
c *Der Unterricht in der Schule und die Gesetze.*
d *Weil sie nach SED-Politikern und anderen Kommunisten genannt wurden.*
e *Arbeitslosigkeit*
f *Sie verstehen einander nicht gut, und die Ostdeutschen haben da Gefühl, als Bürger zweiter Klasse behandelt zu werden.*
g *Die Leute hatten vierzig Jahre lang nichts miteinander zu tun und lebten unter völlig verschiedenen politischen Systemen.*

p 84, activity 2

Interviewerin: Also Thomas, wie alt waren Sie im Jahre 1990?
Thomas: Ich war damals 15 Jahre alt.Interviewerin: Und wie hat sich das Leben in den neuen Bundesländern verändert?
Thomas: Fast alles ist anders heutzutage. Ich beginne bei den guten Sachen: die Demokratie natürlich und auch die Reisefreiheit. Ich bin in den letzten Jahren unter anderem nach Spanien, Italien, und Amerika gefahren. Von so was konnten

	meine Eltern nur noch träumen. Auch können wir Produkte kaufen, die es vorher bei uns überhaupt nicht gab – schöne Autos, Markenklamotten, sogar Nahrungsmittel wie Bananen.
Interviewerin:	Gibt es noch andere Vorteile?
Thomas:	Ja, vor allem muss man keine Angst mehr vor der Stasi haben.
Interviewerin:	Was ist denn die Stasi?
Thomas:	Der Staatssicherheitsdienst. Das war wie der KGB in der Sowjetunion. Sie haben den Leuten nachspioniert, um sich zu vergewissern, dass man nichts unternommen hatte, was gegen den kommunistischen Staat war.
Interviewerin:	Die Wende hat also viel Positives gebracht. Aber war das am Anfang nicht ziemlich verwirrend?
Thomas:	Ja, ich war damals in der Schule und auf einmal gab es ein völlig neues Schulsystem. Auch die Lehrer wussten nicht so richtig, was sie unterrichten sollten. Alle Gesetze waren neu – man lebte also eine Zeitlang in Unsicherheit, weil nichts mehr so war, wie wir es gewöhnt waren. Selbst die Namen von den Straßen und Städten haben sich geändert. Karl-Marx-Stadt wurde wieder Chemnitz und in meiner Stadt hieß Wilhelm-Pieck-Straße plötzlich Theaterstraße.
Interviewerin:	Und warum hat man das gemacht?
Thomas:	Na, Wilhelm Pieck war ein SED-Politiker, er musste also weg!
Interviewerin:	Hat die Wende auch Nachteile gebracht?
Thomas:	Ja, Arbeitslosigkeit. In der DDR konnte man kaum reich werden, aber jeder hatte einen Arbeitsplatz. Unsere Industrie ist aber veraltet und ist in der freien Marktwirtschaft keineswegs konkurrenzfähig. Für Jugendliche war es besonders schwierig, keine Perspektive zu haben. Ich habe in Weimar studiert, musste aber nach Frankfurt ziehen, um eine Stelle zu bekommen. Ein zweites Problem ist, dass die DDR-Bürger oft meinen, sie werden von den Westdeutschen als Bürger zweiter Klasse behandelt.
Interviewerin:	Verstehen sich die West- und Ostdeutschen denn gar nicht?
Thomas:	Es ist vielleicht übertrieben zu sagen, man versteht sich nicht, aber man spricht immer noch von der „Mauer in den Köpfen", auch von „Ossis" und „Wessis". Ich finde das auch selbstverständlich. Die Leute hatten vierzig Jahre lang nichts miteinander zu tun und lebten unter völlig verschiedenen politischen Systemen. Es wird also ein bisschen dauern, bis wir uns wiede wie ein Volk fühlen.
Interviewerin:	Thomas, danke für das Gespräch.

3a Students read the text.

3b Students answer the questions in German to check their understanding of the text.

Answers:

a *Ossis und Wessis / Mauer im Kopf*
b *der wirtschaftliche Unterschied zwischen Ost und West*
c *blühende Landschaften / Wohlhaben im Osten*
d *Es war die Verkopplung eines modernen Industriestaats mit einem armen Land.*
e *Es gibt keine Infrastruktur. / Es ist zu teuer.*
f *Arbeitslosigkeit / dreimal so hoch wie im Westen*
g *Beide haben ihre Jobs verloren. / Er hat jetzt einen Job in München. / leben getrennt*
h *Drogen / Die Jugend zieht weg.*

4 Students listen to the interview with Katja Sulzer and choose the correct answer.

Answers:

a 1 **b** 2 **c** 1 **d** 3 **e** 3 **f** 1

p 85, activity 4

Int:	Katja, du warst noch sehr klein, als die Mauer fiel. Was weißt du über das Leben in der DDR?
Katja:	Ich habe das persönlich nicht erlebt, aber meine Eltern haben viel davon erzählt. Und ich habe Filme wie ‚Goodbye Lenin' und ‚Das Leben der Anderen' gesehen, die einen guten Einblick in das damalige Leben geben. Aber meine Mutter regt sich manchmal auf, weil sie meint, dass wir nur was von der schlechten Seite der DDR erfahren. Es gab auch gute Sachen, meint sie, wie Haushaltstage für arbeitende Mütter, gute Sozialeinrichtungen, kostenlose Kinderpflege und keine Arbeitslosigkeit. Damals haben sie viel vom Staat bekommen, wofür man jetzt selbst zahlen muss.

Int:	Glaubst du, dass es noch viele Unterschiede zwischen Ossis und Wessis gibt?
Katja:	Unter den Jugendlichen gibt es weniger. Aber Arbeitslosigkeit ist immer noch ein großes Problem im Osten – es ist uns bewusst, dass wir im ärmeren Teil Deutschlands leben.
Int:	Hast du persönliche Erfahrungen damit?
Katja:	Ja, meine Tante hat damals ihren Job verloren und nie wieder was gefunden. Mein Onkel war Lehrer für Russisch, mit Englisch als zweitem Fach, obwohl er vor der Wende nie in einem englischsprachigen Land gewesen war. Er hat umschulen müssen, weil niemand mehr Russisch lernen wollte. Er hat dann als Englischlehrer weitergemacht.
Int:	Bist du deswegen nach Westdeutschland gekommen, um zu studieren?
Katja:	Ja, teilweise. Aber auch, weil das Studium hier mir sehr gut gefiel.
Int:	Glaubst du, dass du in Westdeutschland bleiben wirst?
Katja:	Das kommt darauf an, wo ich nach dem Studium einen Arbeitsplatz finde. Eigentlich würde ich schon gern in der Nähe von zu Hause wohnen. In meinem Dorf gibt es nichts – die jungen Leute gehen alle weg. Aber vielleicht wäre in Leipzig oder in Weimar was zu finden.

5 Students play the part of relatives, one from the former FRG, the other from the former GDR. They explain to their relative what their life is like.

6 Students play the part of an *Ossi* and write a letter about 150 words to relatives in the former West Germany, describing how their life has changed since the fall of the Berlin wall.

Deutschsprachige Länder und Europa

Materials

- Students' Book pages 86–87
- CD 2, tracks 16–17
- *Arbeitsblätter* 36, 37, 38, 39

1 Students complete the quiz about Europe by deciding whether each statement is true (R) or false (F).

Answers:

a *F – 27*
b *R*
c *F – 1951*
d *R*
e *F – 2002*
f *F – die Schweiz nicht*
g *R*
h *R*
i *F*
j *R (Beethovens 9. Symphonie)*

2 Students listen to the report on the expansion of the EU and choose the five statements that are true.

Answers:

a, b, d, f, g

p 86, activity 2

Seit der EU-Erweiterung stehen die deutschsprachigen Länder im Mittelpunkt Europas. Deutschland selbst hat die größte Bevölkerung aller EU-Länder, Deutsch ist die vorherrschende Sprache der Union.

Klar ist, dass die EU-Erweiterung Unbehagen verursacht hat. Die Angst vor einer Flut an Arbeitskräften aus den Ostblockländern, vor allem aus Polen, hat die Regierung dazu geführt, Migrationsquoten einzuführen. Doch der Beitritt des Ostblocks bietet vor allem jungen Deutschsprachigen Chancen. Im Ostblock werden Deutsch und Englisch allgemein als Fremdsprachen gelernt – und wer beides kann, wird gern eingestellt.

Viele Firmen suchen jetzt neue Märkte im Osten. Franziska Herzog arbeitet bei einer deutschen Investionsbank, die gerade eine Filiale in Warschau eröffnet hat. Die Bank bietet Firmen, die nach Polen umsiedeln, Investionen an und stellt Arbeitnehmer aus den beiden Ländern ein. „Die Ostblockländer bieten gute Möglichkeiten für Firmen. Die Löhne und andere Kosten sind niedriger als im Westen. Und die neuen EU-Länder brauchen Unterstützung – wir haben viele mehr Erfahrung in der Marktwirtschaft ", meint sie. Jan Borowski aus Krakau arbeitet bei derselben Bank, aber in Wien. Hier verbessert er seine Deutschkenntnisse und lernt alles über das Bankwesen. Nach zwei Jahren wird er nach Polen zurückkommen. Ohne die EU-Erweiterung hätte er diese Ausbildung nie bekommen. „Zwischen Deutschland und Polen gibt es eine unglückliche Gechichte", sagt er. „Aber jetzt gehören wir beide zur größten Wirtschaftsmacht der Welt – der EU. Hoffentlich werden wir zusammen für eine bessere Zukunft arbeiten können."

3a Students read the article about the Euro.

3b Students read the article again and make notes on the effects the Euro has had under the categories listed.

3c Students complete the sentences.

Answers:

a *...sehnt sich ein Drittel immer noch zur guten alten D-Mark zurück.*
b *...dass das neue Geld ein „Teuro" sei.*
c *...die zweitwichtigste Währung der Welt.*
d *...inzwischen ein Drittel des Bruttoinlandsprodukts.*
e *...begehren den Euro.*
f *...scheinen sie ihren Vorbehalt aufgeben zu wollen.*

4a Students listen to the conversation and attribute each sentence (a–i) to the appropriate person.

Answers:
Ben: a, e, h Anke: c, d, i Katja: e Jean-Paul: b, g, f

p 87, activity 4a

Anke: Wie realistisch ist eine europäische Kultur? Was meinst du, Ben?
Ben: Ich weiß nicht, ob es wirklich wichtig ist, dass es eine europäische Kultur gibt. Ich finde Europa interessant, gerade weil es verschiedene Kulturen gibt.
Anke: Das finde ich auch. Ich interessiere mich total für andere europäische Länder, die Lebensweisen, die Traditionen und so. So entwickelt man ein europäisches Bewusstsein, und für mich ist das wichtig, und zwar ohne seine eigene Kultur aufzugeben.
Katja: Da stimmt ich dir voll zu, Anke. Es bedeutet auch, dass man europäisch denkt, und so kann man hoffentlich auch in Zukunft den Frieden erhalten, gemeinsam gegen Rassismus kämpfen und so.
Jean-Paul: Ja, aber Katja, ein Land sollte jedoch seine Eigenheiten nie ganz aufgeben. Ich persönlich finde auch den europäischen Fernsehkanal Arte gut. Er zeigt interessante Filme und Dokumentationen in Französisch und Deutsch. Aber ich würde nicht sagen, ich bin Europäer, sondern immer noch Franzose. Anke, du hast die Frage gestellt, wie ist deine Meinung?
Anke: Ja, sowie Jean-Paul finde ich ausländische Filme total gut oder auch Ausstellungen mit Bildern von ausländischen Künstlern. Man lernt andere Menschen besser verstehen, wie –
Ben: Genau, oh sorry.
Anke: Wie sie denken, worüber sie lachen, zum Beispiel. OK, Ben, du bist daran.
Ben: Ja, genau, und so entwickelt sich tolerantes Denken und Handeln. Meiner Meinung nach ist das europäisches Bewusstsein. Das ist wichtiger als eine einheitliche europäische Kultur. Auch wenn man die Partnerschaften zwischen europäischen Städten und Schulen unterstützt, zeigt das ein europäisches Bewusstsein.
Alle: Doch, das stimmt.

4b Students pick out examples from the listening text to demonstrate that they show a European awareness.

5a Students discuss the topics listed with a partner.

5b Students now write up their discussion.

Prüfungstraining

Grammar and skills

- Describing some German festivals
- Answering questions correctly in German
- *Arbeitsblatt* 40

Materials

- Students' Book pages 88–89
- CD 2, track 18

1 As an introduction to this spread, students match the dates to festivals.

Answers:
a 4 **b** 10 **c** 1 **d** 9 **e** 2 **f** 8 **g** 5 **h** 7 **i** 3 **j** 6

2a Students read the texts about three different festivals in German speaking countries.

2b Students find synonyms for the words a–h in the three texts.

Answers:

a *sich vermummen*
b *die Macht*
c *die Fastenzeit*
d *wachsen*
e *Maßkrug*
f *Rummelplatz*
g *ums Leben kommen*
h *entsorgen*

2c Students answer the questions in German to test their comprehension.

Answers:

a *man wollte die bösen Geister des Winters vertreiben*
b *am Samstag vor Aschermittwoch*
c *ein Kostüm*
d *Touristen*
e *ein kleines Bier*
f *Achterbahnen und Karussells/ein Rummelplatz*
g *Sie hat alle Rekorde gebrochen.*
h *Ein Mann ist ums Leben gekommen.*
i *Kreislaufprobleme und Knochenbrüche*
j *Die Stadt musste gereinigt werden.*

3 Students listen to the report about *Fastnacht* and the *Oktoberfest* and answer the questions.

Answers:

a *die Macht*
b *Bürger der Stadt*
c *mit einem Riesenfest*
d *ein großer Umzug durch die Stadt*
e *alle sind in Urlaubsstimmung; alle können mitmachen*
f *wie groß es ist*
g *zu viele Touristen, zu kommerziell*
h *weil man da jeden kennt*

p 89, activity 3

Christian:	Also, ich wohne in Aulendorf, das ist eine kleine Stadt in Oberschwaben, aber bei uns wird die Fastnacht, oder Fasnet, wie wir sie nennen, groß gefeiert. Bei uns beginnt sie eigentlich schon am Donnerstag.
Int:	Was, am Donnerstag schon?
Christian:	Ja, ich glaube im Rheinland ist es ein bisschen anders, aber bei uns geht es schon früher los, dann bekommen die Narren die Schlüssel der Stadt.
Int:	Und wer sind diese Narren?
Christian:	Das sind alle Bürger der Stadt. Sie sind halt in Narrenzunft und dann bei der Fasnet spielen sie die Narren. So lange die Narren an der Macht sind, ist das Leben anders als sonst.
Int:	Und was passiert?
Christian:	Das ist einfach ein großes Fest. Am Samstag findet immer ein Riesenfest in der Stadthalle statt. Da wird meistens sehr viel getrunken und man soll sich verkleiden, als Mönch oder so was. Dann am Montag geht ein großer Umzug durch die Stadt.
Int:	Das macht bestimmt Spaß.
Christian:	Ja, es ist schön, weil alle Urlaubsstimmung haben und auch weil alle mitmachen können. Es gibt Sachen für die Kinder und für die Erwachsenen.
Int:	Und warst du schon auf dem Oktoberfest?
Christian:	Ja, vor zwei Jahren. Ein Freund von mir war schon dabei gewesen und hat gemeint, es sei sehr lustig. Das hat schon was und es ist imponierend, wie groß das ist. Wir sind Achterbahn gefahren und haben auch in einem großen Zelt gesessen und haben Bier getrunken und geplaudert.
Int:	Würdest du noch mal hingehen?
Christian:	Es war schon interessant, da zu sehen, aber nein, ich werde nicht noch mal hingehen. Ich finde, es ist sehr kommerziell geworden, es gibt wahnsinnig viele Touristen und es ist auch ziemlich teuer. Ich finde unser eigenes Stadtfest eigentlich gemütlicher. Da kennst du jeden und kannst einfach mit den Bürgern deiner eigenen Stadt feiern.

4 Students do more research about one of the three festivals in order to give a talk to the class. Useful websites are listed in the Students' Book.

5 Students imagine they have been to one of the three festivals and write up a report about the event. This could be done for homework.

Zur Auswahl

Materials

- Students' Book page 90
- Solo CD, tracks 9–10

S 

1 Students listen and make notes.

Answers:

a *„Sokrates": mehrwöchiges Auslandspraktikum; „Ausbildungsbrücke": ermöglicht Auszubildenden ein Praktikum in einem anderen Land; der Europass: Auskunft über Ausbildungs- oder Weiterbildungsmöglichkeiten und Qualifikationen*

b *das Erasmusprogramm: an einer Uni in einem anderen Land studieren; Fremdsprachenassistent an einer Schule; Europa-Kolleg in Brügge: europäische Ausbildung*

p 90, activity 1

(telephone conversation)

Hallo. Guten Tag. Wie kann ich Ihnen helfen?... Aha, Sie hätten gern Informationen über Arbeitsmöglichkeiten für Jugendliche in der EU. Nun, da gibt es verschiedene Programme. Zum einen gibt es das Bildungsprogramm „Sokrates". Dieses Programm bietet europäischen Jugendlichen die Möglichkeit, eines mehrwöchigen Auslandpraktikums. Ein Beispiel wäre ein Praktikum an einer Grundschule mit dem Ziel, die Schüler über Ihr Land zu informieren und so europäisches B ewusstsein zu fördern.

Dann gibt es auch noch ein Programm speziell für junge Auszubildende. Es heißt „Ausbildungsbrücke" und ermöglicht interessierten Jugendlichen ein Praktikum in einer Firma oder einem Unternehmen in einem europäischen Partnerland.

Drittens wäre da der Europass. Er gibt Auskunft über Ausbildungs- oder Weiterbildungsmöglichkeiten, sowie über europäische Qualifikationen in EU-Staaten. Wie bitte? Programme für Studenten?

Ja sicher, gibt es auch. Als erstes wäre da das Erasmusprogramm zu nennen. Es bietet Studenten die Möglichkeit an einer Schule zu arbeiten. Das ist auch ein sehr beliebtes Programm. Vielleicht haben Sie schon einmal etwas vom Europa-Kolleg in Brügge gehört? Es bietet 260 Studenten ein Intensivstudium, eine europäische Ausbildung. Das Ziel ist es, europäisches Denken und Handeln zu fördern.

... Ja, ich kann Ihnen Informationsmaterial über diese Programme schicken. Kein Problem. Wie ist Ihr Name?

2a Students read the text about cooperation between member EU countries.

2b Students summarise the text, using the bullet points to make sure they cover everything important.

S

3 Students listen to a report about East Germans who tried to escape from the former East Germany and then they answer the questions in German.

Answers:

a *über 5000*

b *Um das ständig perfektionierte DDR-Grenzsicherungssystem zu überwinden.*

c *Heißluftballons, umgebaute Autos, sogar ein Mini-U-Boot, und eine Lautsprecherbox.*

d *57 Personen sind durch den erfolgreichsten Tunnel nach Westberlin gekommen.*

e *In den 28 Jahren ihres Bestehens sind 239 Personen an der Mauer gestorben.*

f *Er sprang aus einem Fenster in der Bernauer Straße.*

g *Er wurde erschossen und lag schwer verwundet und blutend am Fuße der Mauer, ohne dass jemand ihm half.*

h *Er wurde erschossen.*

p 90, activity 3

Über 5000 Menschen gelang zwischen 1961 und 1989 die Flucht über die Mauer. Not macht erfinderisch! Die Hilfsmitteln wurden im Laufe der Jahre immer ausgefeilter, um das ständig perfektionierte DDR-Grenzsicherungssystem zu überwinden. Manche benutzen Heißluftballons, umgebaute Autos, sogar ein Mini-U-Boot wurde als Fluchmittel verwendet. Auch in einer Lautsprecherbox wurde aus der DDR geflüchtet. Zahlreiche Fluchttunnels wur

den gebaut. An zwei Abenden im Oktober 1964 sind 57 Personen durch
den erfolgreichsten Tunnel nach Westberlin gekommen. Das Risiko war jedoch groß, dass die Mauer ihre Opfer verlangte. In den 28 Jahren ihre Bestehens starben 239 Personen an der Mauer, die von Grenzposten erschossen wurden, in der Spree ertranken, oder aus Fenstern in den Tod sprangen. Das erste Opfer war Rudolf Urban, der am 19. August 1961 bei seinem Sprung aus einem Fenster in der Bernauer Straße ums Leben kam. Ein Jahr später schockierte der Tod des jungen Peter Fechter die Welt. Er wurde erschossen und lag schwer verwundet und blutend am Fuße der Mauer, ohne dass ihm jemand half. Der letzte an der Mauer ermordete Flüchtling war der junge Chris Gueffroy, der am 6. Februar 1989 erschossen wurde.

4 Students choose one of the subjects listed to research and prepare a talk to give to the class.

Wiederholung Einheit 7–8

Materials

- Students' Book, pages 91–92
- CD 2, track 19

1 Students listen to the recording and answer the questions in English.

Answers:

a *The market has risen for the past three years.*
b *There is mix of all sorts of books, including translations of bestsellers.*
c *a steady growth*
d *independent retailers*
e *doesn't have a big stock/customers who used to order from him now buy online instead*
f *reduce prices*
g *offers a different shopping experience/with a seating area for reading/and a wine bar*

p 91, activity 1

Deutschland ist im Lesefieber: der Bücherumsatz in Deutschland ist wie in den beiden Vorjahren gestiegen, diesmal um 3%, trotz einer Erhöhung des Durchschnittspreises. Ein Blick auf die Bestsellerliste zeigt eine gute Mischung aus allen Kategorien: Krimis scheinen bei den Deutschen besonders gut anzukommen; lustige Geschichten, historische Romane und Selbsthilfebücher sind auch gut vertreten. Auch der Geschmack der Deutschen ist international – viele der Besteller sind aus anderen Sprachen übersetzt. Dass der Markt so gesund ist, ist für die Buchhändler eine willkommene Nachricht, aber auch die Online-Umsätze wachsen stetig und machen inzwischen 12% des Marktes aus. Der Erfolg der Online-Buchhändler geht oft zu Lasten der unabhängigen Buchhändler, vor allem kleiner Buchläden. Ralf Zimmermann ist Besitzer einer Buchhandlung in einer bayerischen Kleinstadt. Er hat keine großen Mengen in seinem Laden, aber früher hatten Kunden die gewünschten Bücher bei ihm bestellt.

Da viele seiner Kunden das nun selber im Internet machen, macht er Verluste. Dass der Marktanteil von Online-Buchhandlungen noch nicht größer ist, hängt mit der Buchpreisbindung zusammen. Im Vergleich zu anderen Ländern müssen Online-Buchhändler in Deutschland die Bücher zum selben Preis wie jeder andere Buchhändler anbieten.

Thomas Schröder, Besitzer einer Buchhandlung in der Nähe vom amazon-Versandzentrum in Bad Helsen, sollte wie andere unabhängige Buchhändler Angst vor Online-Rivalen haben. Er vertraut aber auf etwas in seinem Laden, dass das Internet niemals anbieten kann: eine Sitzecke, wo Kunden lesen können, und eine Weinstube. Er glaubt, dadurch ein ganz anderes Einkaufserlebnis bieten zu können, und hofft, damit die Zukunft seiner Buchhandlung zu sichern.

2a Students read the text.

2b A reading comprehension activity. Students answer the questions on the reading text in German.

Answers:

a *ihre Bücher direkt verkaufen/veröffentlichen*
b *Bücher werden erst gedruckt, wenn sie bestellt werden/Es gibt kein Lager, nur einen Raum mit Druckern.*
c *Sie hat keinen Verlag gefunden.*
d *Preis/Aussehen/Verdienst*
e *Wunsch ihrer sterbenden Tochter*
f *spenden an die Kinderkrebshilfe*
g *Konkurrenz/Verlage wollen keine Risiken eingehen*
h *Erfolg von Büchern, die von Verlagen abgelehnt wurden*

3 Students work with a partner to discuss whether they prefer to buy books online or in book shops and why and what they think of the website, *Bücher auf Nachfrage*, featured in the reading text.

4a Students read the text, *Das Leben der Anderen.*

4b Students read the first paragraph again and then choose the correct answer.

Answers:

a 3 **b** 1 **c** 1

4c Students read the second and third paragraphs again and decide which four of the statements listed are correct.

Answers:

a, c, e, g

4d Students translate the last paragraph.

Possible answer:

In Das Leben der Anderen, *Dreyman also decides to read his file as he, like many other GDR citizens, wants to understand his own past.*

Politik – Globale Probleme
Einheit 9

Unit objectives

By the end of this unit students will be able to:

- Understand the German political system and the latest national and international developments
- Discuss the rights of the individual in a democracy
- Work out the meaning of war and terrorism

Grammar

By the end of this unit students will be able to:

- Use conjunctions
- Use relative pronouns

Skills

By the end of this unit students will be able to:

- Link sentences grammatically and logically

Materials

- Students' Book pages 93

1 Students match the beginnings of the sentences with the endings.

Answers:
1 e 2 a 3 c

2a Students work with a partner and in two minutes list in English everything they already know about English politics.

2b Students use the Internet to research German politics. They should use the photos in the Students' Book as a starting point. They then give a one-minute presentation to the rest of the class.

Politik – national und international

Materials

- Students' Book pages 94–95
- CD 2, track 20
- *Arbeitsblätter* 41, 42, 43

1a Students carry out a mind-mapping exercise with their partner and note all terms to do with German politics which they already know.

1b They now compare notes with their fellow students and compile an even bigger list with the aid of a dictionary.

2a Students read the text *Was ist bloß aus dem Mädchen geworden?* about Angela Merkel.

2b Students complete sentences with information based on the reading text in 2a.

Answers:

a *nicht katholisch, geschieden, eine Frau, aus Ostdeutschland*
b *ihr Vater Pfarrer war*
c *sie Physik studierte*
d *der Akademie der Wissenschaften in Berlin*
e *in der Politik tätig gewesen war*

3a Students listen to the discussion about Angela Merkel.

p 94, activities 3a and 3b

Thea Sommer, Mitglied der Jungen Union

Also ich finde es einfach toll, was die Bundeskanzlerin erreicht hat. Wissen Sie, wir hatten schon mal eine große Koalition, 1966, und die hielt nur drei Jahre. Doch heute haben wir zum ersten Mal seit der Wende eine richtig starke Regierung, die auch Entscheidungen treffen kann. Durch ihren Einsatz hat Frau Merkel erreicht, dass die Arbeitslosenquote erheblich gesunken ist und auch, dass Amerika umweltbewusster geworden ist. Angela Merkel ist ein tolles Vorbild für die deutsche Jugend und für mich ist es besonders wichtig zu sehen, dass man auch als Frau Erfolg haben kann.

Udo Winkler, Mitglied der Neuen Linken

Nun, es kommt mir doch ganz merkwürdig vor, dass jemand, der bis Mitte Dreißig nie Demokratie erlebt hat, plötzlich zum Staatsoberhaupt werden kann. Angela Merkel ist schließlich in der DDR aufgewachsen, hat auf Staatskosten studiert und sogar promoviert. Warum hat sie allen sozialistischen Werten den Rücken gekehrt und ist total zum Wessi geworden? Verstehen Sie, ich glaube, diese Frau wollte einfach an die Macht. Andererseits ist es vielleicht gar nicht so schlecht, dass eine aus dem Osten am Ruder ist. Vielleicht versteht sie die Ängste und Probleme besser, die wir Ossis noch haben, und gibt uns wieder, woran wir hier gewöhnt waren, wie kostenlose Kitas und Vollbeschäftigung.

3b Students answer the questions on the listening text.

Answers:

a *eine starke Regierung*
b *die Senkung der Arbeitslosenzahl*
c *das größere amerikanische Engagement beim Umweltschutz*
d *weil sie unbedingt an die Macht wollte*
e *weil sie vielleicht die Ostdeutschen besser versteht*
f *kostenlose Kitas und Vollbeschäftigung*

A 42

4a Students read the text about the electoral gains of the Left and the Right. They should also look at *Arbeitsblatt* 42.

4b Students explain some of the key expressions from the reading text in simple German. This could also be done as pair work or homework.

Answers:

a *nach der Wiedervereinigung / nachdem die Mauer gefallen war*
b *Länder, die früher zur DDR gehörten*
c *mehr Menschen wählten diese Partei*
d *die Tatsache, dass immer mehr Menschen diese Partei gut fanden*

5a Students read the text about the new distribution of power in Europe.

5b Students write an essay of 250–400 words on one of two titles listed.

Die Macht des Einzelnen

Key language

- *sich für ein Anliegen entscheiden*
- *im Internet oder in der Bibliothek nachforschen*
- *Fakten auf einer Liste zusammenstellen*
- *Flugblätter anfertigen*
- *Informationen verteilen*
- *die Presse informieren*
- *eine Unterschriftensammlung organisieren*
- *an die Stadt-/Kreis-/Landesverwaltung schreiben*
- *eine Versammlung zusammenrufen*
- *eine Bürgerinitiative gründen*

Materials

- Students' Book pages 96–97
- CD 2, track 21

1a Students read the statements and study the pictures. They then work with a partner to decide whether or not each group of people in the photos is justified in demonstrating.

1b Students rank the issues listed according to their own priorities and justify their rank order in a few sentences to the rest of the group.

2a Students read the text on NPD activities and how inhabitants of the town of Rheinsberg have reacted to them.

2b Students answer questions on the text in 2a in German.

Answers:

a *Rheinsberg hat ein Schloss, und Verbindungen mit den Schriftstellern Kurt Tucholsky und Theodor Fontane.*
b *Eine Dönerbude wurde in Brand gesteckt und zerstört.*
c *Sie demonstrierten gegen die Täter, begannen eine Spendenaktion.*
d *Weil die NPD Land kaufen wollte.*
e *Als Zentrum, wo sich Rechtsradikale treffen und ausbilden lassen/lernen können.*
f *ein Rockkonzert, eine Plakat- und Transparentaktion*

2c Students explain the expressions, taken from the text, in German, using their own words.

Answers:

a *Sie hätten sich bessere Informationen/Nachrichten in der Presse/Zeitung gewünscht.*
b *Was bedeutete, dass der Inhaber alles/seinen ganzen Besitz verlor.*
c *Damit die Menschen mehr für das Wohl ihrer Mitbürger tun.*
d *Ähnliche Methoden benutzen und dabei gewinnen.*

3a Students listen to the recording about the introduction of night flights and increased noise pollution.

p 97, activities 3a and 3b

Der Energieverbrauch und damit die CO2 Emissionen nehmen in Deutschland pro Jahr um circa dreieinhalb Prozent zu. Wenn die bisherige Entwicklung so weiter geht, werden die Klimaauswirkungen des Fliegens in fünf Jahren die des heutigen PKW-Verkehrs übersteigen. Vermeiden lässt sich eine Katastrophe nur, wenn Kurzstreckenflüge unterbleiben, die vorhandenen Flughäfen nicht weiter ausgebaut werden und die

Passagiere auf die Bahn umsteigen. Derzeit gibt es in Deutschland 257 Flughäfen, darunter Frankfurt, mit immerhin 53 Millionen Passagieren der drittgrößte Flughafen Europas. Damit hat Deutschland bereits die höchste Flughafendichte der Welt.

Nichtsdestotrotz versuchen die Fluglinien, unter Druck durch ständig steigende Treibstoffkosten, jede Möglichkeit, den Flugverkehr profitabel zu erhalten, auszuschöpfen. Dazu stehen seit kurzem auch Nachtflüge auf dem Programm. Im Jahr 2000 war in Hessen von allen Beteiligten ein Abkommen unterzeichnet worden, das den Nachtflugverkehr von 23 Uhr bis fünf Uhr morgens völlig untersagte.

Jetzt verlangt die Lufthansa in Plänen zur Erweiterung des Frankfurter Flughafens die Erlaubnis für bis zu 150 Nachtflüge.

Ein Skandal, wetterte die Vorstandssprecherin des Bündnisses der Bürgerinitiativen, Brigitte Martin, den Menschen im Großraum Frankfurt sollten pro Nacht mindestens sieben Stunden ungestörten Schlafs zugesichert werden, und Vertreter dieser Initiativen fordern einen sofortigen Bau- und Planungsstopp sowie Mitbeteiligung am Ausbauprojekt.

Nach einer Lärmbelästigungsstudie fühlen sich 40 Prozent aller Hessen durch Fluglärm gestört und mit 75 Dezibel im unmittelbaren Bereich um Frankfurt/Darmstadt sogar sehr stark.

Das Verkehrsministerium überprüft zur Zeit den Antrag der Bürgerinitiativen.

3b Students match the beginnings with the ends of sentences, based on the listening text in 3a. Point out that there are more endings than beginnings.

Answers:
a 3 **b** 7 **c** 4 **d** 6 **e** 2

4a Students work with a partner to compile a list of causes for which they would be prepared to take part in a demonstration.

4b Students design a poster advertising their chosen cause and give a one-minute speech to plead their cause in front of their fellow students.

4c Students describe in 250–400 words how they would organise a campaign to find a solution to their cause, using expressions from the *Hilfe* box to help them. Students could also be encouraged to research the topic further on their own by accessing a relevant German website.

Krieg und Terrorismus

Skills focus

- Improving writing

Key language

- *einen Krieg führen*
- *Atomwaffen einsetzen*
- *mit allen Mitteln verhindern*
- *auf diplomatischem Wege*
- *die Sicherheitskontrolle*
- *seine Schuhe ausziehen müssen*
- *jede Handtasche durchsuchen*

Materials

- Students' Book pages 98–99
- CD 2, track 22

1a Students discuss with a partner which of the three scenarios listed they are most afraid.

1b Students justify their decision in front of the class.

2a Students read the article on Germany's attitude towards military conflicts. This is preparation for the A2 oral examination.

2b Students answer the questions.

Possible answers:

a *In beiden Weltkriegen hat es sehr viele Tote gegeben und die Weltkriege sind von den Deutschen begonnen worden. Jetzt haben die Deutschen ein schlechtes Gewissen, weil so viele Menschen wegen ihrer Politik gestorben sind.*

b *Die Juden sind hauptsächlich während des Zweiten Weltkrieges verfolgt worden. Sie starben zur selben Zeit wie viele Soldaten und Zivilisten. Deshalb fühlen sich die Deutschen sehr schlecht, weil die Juden wie Zivilisten umgebracht worden sind.*

c *Die Menschen wollten zeigen, dass ein Krieg gegen den Irak nicht gerecht sei und dass sie keinen Krieg wollten.*

d *Die deutschen Soldaten sollen helfen, das Land wieder aufzubauen und die Bevölkerung und ihre eigenen Aufbaumannschaften zu schützen.*

2c Students work in groups and discuss the questions listed.

2d Students read through the text again and make notes under the two headings listed.

3a Students listen to German people giving their opinions on terrorism.

p 98, activities 3a and 3b

Herr Frieda: In den Sechziger und Siebziger Jahren hielt die Baader Meinhof Gruppe ganz Deutschland in Atem. Anfangs konnten wir, ich war zu der Zeit Student, sie noch verstehen. Wir waren alle gegen den Vietnamkrieg und den Materialismus unserer Eltern, doch bald fing es mit den Geiselnahmen und den Ermordungen an und da wurde es ernst. Meine Verlobte arbeitete damals in einer Bank und die hatten alle Angst vor Überfällen. Insgesamt kamen 61 Menschen aufgrund dieser terroristischen Aktivitäten ums Leben.

Susi Frieda: Meine Eltern erzählen mir öfter von dem Terrorismus, als mein Vater noch studierte. Ich war da allerdings noch nicht auf der Welt, deshalb kann ich mir schlecht vorstellen, dass Deutsche anderen Deutschen drohen. Was mich und meine Freunde heutzutage vor allem beschäftigt, ist die Gefahrdurch islamistische Extremisten. Zwar halten wir Deutschen in der U-Bahn keine Ausschau nach Bomben, aber die verschärften Kontrollen an den Flughäfen und Vorfälle im Ausland geben doch uns zu denken. Wir wollten 2004 mit der Schule aus eine Studienreise nach Madrid machen. Die wurde aber abgesagt wegen der Bombenexplosionen. In Hamburg wurden auch Terroristenzellen festgestellt. Mir wäre es jedenfalls echt unangenehm, in derselben Straße wie ein Selbstmordattentäter zu leben.

3b Students answer the questions in English.

Answers:

Herr Frieda:

a *because everyone had demonstrated against their parents' materialism and American politics*

b *when the first people died as a result of the terrorist attacks*

c *61*

Susi Frieda:

d *the Islamic terrorists*

e *tighter security controls at airports and dangers of terrorist attacks when abroad*

f *a school trip to an Art exhibition in Madrid was cancelled*

4a Students read a passage on terrorist cells in Hamburg.

4b Students select the correct answer from three possibilities.

Answers:

a 2 **b** 1 **c** 3

5 Students write an essay of 250–400 words, choosing one of two titles given. Encourage them to use the *Hilfe* box for support.

Prüfungstraining

Grammar and skills

- Understanding how complex sentence structures with subordinate clauses work, using conjunctions
- Using relative pronouns correctly
- Selecting appropriate vocabulary for abstract concepts
- Linking sentences grammatically and logically

Materials

- Students' Book pages 100–101
- Grammar Workbook pages 35, 74, 76
- *Arbeitsblätter* 44, 45

Grammatik

A Students link the sentences using the conjunction given in brackets. Refer them to the grammar revision box and the section on conjunctions in the grammar section for support.

Answers:

a *Deutschland hat eine starke Regierung, **seitdem** die CDU und die SPD zusammen eine Koalition gebildet **haben**.*

b *Niemand hätte es für möglich gehalten, **dass** eine Ostdeutsche und dazu noch eine Frau Kanzlerin **wird**.*

c *Viele Ostdeutsche haben nach der Wende ihre Arbeitsplätze verloren, **weil** die Betriebe saniert oder sogar geschlossen werden **mussten**.*

d *Die Zahl der Arbeitslosen ist in Deutschland seit 2005 gesunken, **obwohl** die Weltwirtschaftslage prekär **schien**.*

B Students rewrite the sentences, beginning each one with the conjunction.

Answers:

a ***Während*** *in den alten Bundesländern die Grünen die Politik* ***mitbestimmen, sind*** *in den neuen Bundesländern linke Parteien relativ stark vertreten.*

b ***Nachdem*** *erst mal die Berliner Mauer gefallen* ***war, war*** *die Wiedervereinigung Deutschlands nicht aufzuhalten.*

c ***Da*** *die Ostdeutschen von nun an demokratische Rechte* ***genossen, begrüßten*** *viele Menschen die Wende.*

d ***Als*** *sich plötzlich der Preis für Mieten und Brot* ***verdreifachte, sehnten*** *sich andere dagegen nach einer Rückkehr in einen sozialistischen Staat.*

Grammatik

A Students add the missing relative pronoun. Encourage them to use the grammar box and grammar reference section 4.4.1 for support if necessary.

Answers:

a *Dr Helmut Kohl war der Kanzler,* ***der*** *Deutschland vereinigt hat.*

b *Der Bundespräsident,* ***dessen*** *Amtssitz Schloss Bellevue ist, wird alle fünf Jahre gewählt.*

c *Der Reichstag ist das Gebäude, in* ***dem*** *der Bundestag seine Sitzungen abhält.*

d *Nicht alle Ostdeutschen,* ***denen*** *Freiheit und Wohlstand versprochen worden war, sind jetzt mit ihrem Leben zufrieden.*

B Students link the two halves of sentences.

Answers:

a *Die Linke ist eine Partei, in der die ehemaligen ostdeutschen Sozialdemokraten und die extrem linken der SPD zusammengefunden haben.*

b *Die FDP ist eine Partei, ohne die die großen Parteien oft keine Regierung hätten bilden können.*

c *Die NPD ist eine Partei, über die viele politische Beobachter Besorgnis äußern.*

d *Die CSU ist eine Partei, mit der die CDU eine große Fraktion im Bundestag bildet.*

1 Students select the past participle which best fits each sentence.

Answers:

a *verabschiedet*

b *ergriffen*

c *getroffen*

d *gefasst*

2a Students compare two texts on the same theme.

2b Students compile a list of expressions from the second passage which might improve their own writing style.

Possible answers:

es war offensichtlich, dass (value statement)

während des Jahres (reference to time)

... hatten zusehen müssen (suggestion emotion: being powerless)

als, conjunction (linking 2 clauses)

sogar (interpretation of event)

es entsetzte sie (giving opinion)

dass (conjunction, linking 2 clauses)

gestärkt durch die Ereignisse ... (giving reasons for what was happening)

verlangen (stronger verb than wollen)

aus diesem Grund (giving reason, logical link of 2 sentences)

zu aller Erstaunen (value judgement)

und führte dazu ...(giving reason for next sentence)

dass (conj, linking reason with event)

schließlich (giving more information and making value judgement)

3 Students improve the text by joining sentences grammatically and logically. Remind them that they may need to change word order.

Possible answer:

Seitdem die Ölkrise in den Siebziger Jahren das Autofahren teurer machte, wurden die Menschen ohne Zweifel auf ihre Umwelt aufmerksam. Aus diesem Grund bildete sich die Grüne Partei, die den Abbau der Atomkraftwerke und die Einführung umweltschützender Maßnahmen verlangte. Da dies die Industrie viel Geld kostete, war die Partei bei den großen Unternehmern nicht beliebt und auch die breite Masse lehnte sie sogar als unrealistisch ab. Nachdem 1990 der Zusammenschluss mit den Grünen aus dem Osten kam, wurde die Partei stärker und konnte schon 1994 in den Bundestag einziehen. Von 1998 bis 2005 waren sie sogar in der Regierung, weil sich eine Koalition von SPD und den Grünen gebildet hatte.

Zur Auswahl

Skills focus

- Revision of the unit

Materials

- Students' Book page 102
- Solo CD, tracks 11–12

1a Students listen to the report on the work of the Federal Chancellor.

p 102, activities 1a and 1b

Der Präsident der Bundesrepublik Deutschland wird alle fünf Jahre von der Bundesversammlung gewählt.

Seit dem ersten Juli 2004 ist Horst Köhler der neunte Präsident seit Kriegsende. Neben einigen administrativen Funktionen hat der Bundespräsident eher repräsentative Funktione und vertritt die Republik vor allem nach außen.

Im Allgemeinen steht der Bundespräsident über den Parteien und greift nicht direkt ins politische Geschehen ein. Doch ist sein Einfluss als Staatsoberhaupt nicht zu unterschätzen. Genauso hat er das Recht, ein Gesetz nicht zu unterschreiben und dadurch eine Änderung herbeizuführen.

Horst Köhler hatte vor seinem Amtsantritt keine wichtigen politischen Ämter in Deutschland innegehabt und war allein deshalb schon ein idealer Kandidat für das Amt des Präsidenten. Außerdem hatte er an wichtigen europäischen Finanzinstituten gearbeitet, was ihm volkswirtschaftliche Erfahrung eingebracht hat.

Horst Köhler ist beim Volk sehr beliebt, weil er öffentlich Sorgen der Bürger direkt angesprochen hat, wie die Unterschiede zwischen Ost und West, die Arbeitslosigkeit und die Kinderarmut. Manche jedoch kritisieren seine Kommentare als Einmischung in die Politik und die SPD hat bereits für die nächste Wahl eine Gegenkandidatin aufgestellt. Also, bald zwei Frauen an der Spitze Deutschlands?

1b Students answer the questions on the listening text, in German.

Answers:

a *alle fünf Jahre*
b *8*
c *die BRD gegenüber dem Ausland zu repräsentieren*
d *durch Reden/indem er ein Gesetz nicht unterschreibt*
e *er hatte keine politischen Ämter inne/ er hat Erfahrung in der Wirtschaft*
f *Unterschiede zwischen Ost und West/ Arbeitslosigkeit/Kinderarmut*

2a Students work with a partner to prepare definitions of the key expressions from the listening passage.

2b Students then select some of the key expressions and read their definitions to the rest of the class. The class then tries to guess which of the key expressions they are talking about.

3 Students work in pairs or in teams to answer the questions.

Answers:

a *Nationaldemokratische Partei Deutschlands*
b *CDU und SPD*
c *der Bundeskanzler*
d *Alle vier Jahre*
e *Schwarz*
f *Koalition aus der SPD, der FDP und den Grünen*
g *seit (23.Mai) 1999*

4a Students research the term *Verhältniswahlrecht* (proportional representation) and then give a one-minute speech in which they either support or reject this system of allocating votes. Other students try and counter these arguments.

4b Students list arguments in favour of lowering the voting age to 16. They then prepare a speech in which they declare themselves in favour of doing this. The class should find arguments against this proposal in order to keep the status quo.

5 Students listen to the recording and repeat the sentences they hear.

p 102, activities 5

a Sechshundert Bundestagsabgeordnete sitzen im Bundestag.
b Die Bundesversammlung ist das einmalige Zusammenkommen von Bundesrat und Bundestag.
c Viele Bürgerinitiativen sind aus ökologischen Gründen ins Leben gerufen worden.
d Bündnis 90 und die Grünen kümmern sich hauptsächlich um Umweltfragen.
e Die Parteiverdrossenheit ist eine Herausforderung an die Demokratie.

Wiederholung Einheit 9

Materials

- Students' Book pages 103–104
- CD 2, track 23

1a Students read a text on the German Reichstag.

1b Students translate the first and second paragraphs into English.

Answer:
Historically important and highly contested, the new Reichstag in Berlin was reopened in April 1999.

After a construction period of ten years, it had been handed over to Parliament in 1894 in a ceremony. In 1918, Scheidemann announced the Republic from one of its windows. Later on, it was considered a symbol of their increasing power by the National Socialists. On 27th February 1933, it was engulfed in flames which Hitler presumably exploited to ban the Communist party.

1c Students explain expressions from paragraph three in German in their own words.

Possible answers:
- **a** *Die Menschen benutzten das Gebäude, um die Kriegsverletzten und die Kranken zu pflegen.*
- **b** *dort wurde schwer gekämpft*
- **c** *die russischen Soldaten*
- **d** *es war sehr wichtig für sie/es bedeutete ihnen sehr viel*

1d Students complete the sentences using information from the text.

Answers:
- **a** *... den Umzug der Regierung und der Hauptstadt nach Berlin.*
- **b** *... mit der Restaurierung des Reichstags beauftragt wurde/die Restaurierung des Reichstags vornahm.*
- **c** *... der Reichstag wiedereröffnet/dem Parlament übergeben.*
- **d** *... der deutschen Regierung beim Arbeiten zusehen.*

2a Students listen to report on the former minister for Agriculture, Renate Künast.

p 104, activities 2a and 2b

Renate Künast hat viele Gesichter:
Mal rollt sie auf Skates durch das Brandenburger Tor, ein andermal steht sie mit Gummistiefeln auf einem Bauernhof im Matsch oder sitzt mit ihren Kollegen am Verhandlungstisch.

Frau Künast hat zuerst Sozialfürsorge und später Jura studiert. Sie hat sich in ihrem Leben immer für Menschen in Not eingesetzt, wie zum Beispiel ihr Einsatz in einem Berliner Gefängnis und ihre Arbeit mit Drogenabhängigen zeigt.

1979 ist den Grünen beigetreten und arbeitet seitdem für die Partei. Sie war von Januar 2001 bis zum 4. Oktober 2005 Bundesministerin für Verbraucherschutz, Ernährung und Landwirtschaft. Seit dem 18. Oktober 2005 ist sie Fraktionsvorsitzende der Bundestagsfraktion von Bündnis 90/Die Grünen.

Neben der üblichen grünen Agenda wie Umweltschutz und Ausstieg aus der Atomenergie vertritt sie hauptsächlich eine nachhaltige Landwirtschaft. Auch Verbraucherschutz und die Förderung von fairem Handel liegen ihr besonders am Herzen und sie ist pausenlos im Einsatz für eine bessere Welt.

Hierzu Renate Künast **selbst:**
„Wir brauchen konkrete und verbindliche Regeln für die Landwirtschaft und den Anbau von Bioenergien: Wir sollten nur dann importieren, wenn mit einer Zertifizierung der nachhaltige Anbau und der Schutz der Tropenwälder gesichert sind. Monsanto darf nicht zum Microsoft der Welternährung werden. Die Völker in den Entwicklungsländern dürfen nicht von Pharmakonzernen beraubt werden. Und Deutschland muss dafür sorgen, dass der Tropenwald erhalten wird."

Bleibt ihr bei all der politischen Arbeit auch noch Zeit, das Leben zu genießen?
„Ich genieße meine Arbeit, aber ich weiß auch, dass es wichtig ist, ab und zu mal total abzuschalten. aber ich muss dann irgendwie aufs Land raus und skaten, zumindest raus aus diesem Tempo in Berlin. Und wenn es für ein ganzes Wochenende Ausspannen mal nicht reicht, dann gibt es immer noch mein Lieblingsrestaurant, die Trattoria A' Muntagnola in der Fuggerstraße in Schöneberg. Dort kann man wunderbar mit Freunden klönen und die Grünen fühlen sich alle da wie in ihrem eigenen Wohnzimmer."

Die Fraktionsvorsitzende der Grünen hat schon viel erreicht und wir werden in der Zukunft ganz sicher noch mehr von ihr hören.

2b Students answer questions on the listening passage in English to check that they have fully understood it.

Possible answers:
- **a** *because she can be seen skating through Berlin or wading in wellingtons through the mud of a farm*
- **b** *that she is a person who cares about people in distress*
- **c** *leader of the parliamentary Bündnis 90/Green party and Minister for consumer protection, food and agriculture*

d *green issues like environmental protection, phasing out nuclear energy, sustainable agriculture, consumer protection and promotion of fairtrade*

e *it would guarantee that the food does not interfere with the sustainability of the tropical rain forests*

f *rob them*

g *going out into the countryside or going inline skating*

h *she goes to her favourite Italian restaurant in Schöneberg and chats to friends*

3a Students study the table with the results of the last federal election.

3b Students make notes on the table in preparation for a two-minute talk about it. They concentrate particularly on voter turn-out, the number of seats and the possibilities for a coalition government.

3c Students research on the Internet the topic of second votes, *Zweitstimmen*, in the German electoral system. They speculate to what extent this feature may have influenced the outcome of the elections, especially for parties like the FDP.

Stretch and Challenge

1 Umweltverschmutzung

Skills focus

- Improving spoken and written German using 'fillers'

Materials

- Students' Book page 105

1a Students read the text.

1b Students answer the questions on the text.

Answers:

a *um Käufer und Vermieter über den Energiestandard und die Umwelteigenschaften eines Gebäudes zu informieren*

b *Neue Vermieter und Käufer wissen, wie hoch bzw. wie niedrig der Energieverbrauch und die Heizungskosten eines Hauses oder einer Wohnung sind, bevor sie sich dafür entscheiden.*

c *eigene Meinung*

1c Students read the text again and note down 'fillers'.

Answers:
schon, aber, nun, gerade, schon, erst

1d Students translate the sentences containing the 'fillers' into English.

Answers:
For buildings built since 2002, an energy card is already required.

Well, what should the purpose of an energy card really be?

And how do you get one of these energy cards now?

...If there had been energy cards in those days, I probably wouldn't have moved in in the first place," said Mrs Meier from Merzhausen.

2 Students complete the sentences with the appropriate 'filler'.

Answers:

a *aber*

b *denn*

c *eben*

d *nun*

e *nur*

f *doch*

3 Students write a letter to their local newspaper complaining about the amount of energy wasted in our society. They should write 250 words and try to use some 'fillers'.

2 Umweltschutz

Skills focus

- Using 'unless' or *es sei denn, (dass)*

Materials

- Students' Book page 106

1 Students translate the sentences into German.

Answers:

a *Die steigenden Treibhausemissionen von Flugzeugen werden noch mehr Verschmutzung verursachen, es sei denn, es werden Maßnahmen ergriffen, um die Emissionen zu kontrollieren.*

b *Wir werden nicht genug Müllgruben haben, es sei denn, wir recyceln mehr und produzieren weniger Abfall.*

c *Wir werden unseren zukünftigen Energiebedarf nicht decken können, es sei denn, wir investieren mehr in alternative Energiequellen.*

d *Ich werde nicht mit dir einkaufen gehen, es sei denn, du benutzt deine eigenen Tüten.*

2a Students translate the paragraph into English.

Possible answer:
Climate politics regarding air traffic
Since the early 70's, air traffic has increased fivefold. Globally, this meant a huge growth in airlines. According to experts, this growth is to continue over the next 50 years. In Germany alone, the number of people flying has doubled in the last 12 years. This doesn't make for a good prognosis. In order to get to grips with the problem of the constantly increasing CO_2 emissions of air traffic, political solutions must be found. As air traffic is largely an international economic feature, negotiations on an international level are necessary/required. At the same time, there is concern that effective negotiations with regard to climate policies are not to be expected in the near future.

2b Students complete the sentences.

Answers:
a *... dass der Flugverkehr auch in den nächsten fünfzig Jahren weiter wachsen/steigen wird.*
b *... nur politisch/auf politischem Weg gelöst werden.*
c *... erfordert Verhandlungen auf internationaler Ebene.*
d *... werden nicht so schnell zu erwarten sein/wird man nicht so schnell erwarten.*

3 Students read the quote and then write between 250 and 400 words saying to what extent they agree with it.

3 Ausländer

Grammar focus
- Using the subjunctive in negative contexts and temporal clauses
- Using the imperfect or pluperfect subjunctive in subordinate clauses

Materials
- Students' Book page 107
- Grammar Workbook page 59

1 Students translate the sentences into German.

Answers:
a *Die Frage war zu wichtig, als dass die Politiker sie ignoriert hätten.*
b *Hat sie die deutsche Staatsangehörigkeit? Nicht dass ich wüsste.*
c *Statt dass er ihre Fragen beantwortet hätte, schickte er sie zu einem anderen Büro.*

2 Students translate the sentences into German.

Answers:
a *Sie wollten, dass ich zu Hause wartete, bis sie mich abholten.*
b *Wir hätten den Bewerbungstermin beinahe/fast verpasst.*
c *Der Arbeitgeber gab ihm keine Arbeit, bis er die Landessprache lernte.*

3a Students read the text on the subject of immigration and then translate it into English.

Possible answer:
From 1 January 2009, immigration from abroad is to become easier for top professionals. This was decided by the German Cabinet, after home secretary Wolfgang Schäuble and the minister for employment, Olaf Scholz, had put forward an action programme in order to halt the growing lack of experts in the German economy. It is estimated that Germany needs about 400 000 highly qualified employees for the gap to be closed. From 2009, foreign top professionals will be able to work in Germany permanently if they earn at least 63 600 Euro, whereas they had to earn 86 400 Euro so far. However, this ruling does not apply to low- qualified workers from the new eastern European EU-countries. The positive aspect of this ruling is that it will benefit the economic growth without being a burden for the German job market. Simultaneously, the government is trying to encourage the unemployed in Germany to take part in further education until they get a qualification.

According to Schäuble, the government wanted above all to use the potential within the country. How to make the German job market more attractive to foreign top-class professionals is a task which will require a lot of thought from German politicians, as in 2007, the immigration of only 466 top professionals was registered.

3b Students read the text again and decide to what extent they consider this action programme to be a positive thing. They should write about 200 words on this, giving reasons for their views.

4 Armut und Reichtum

Grammar focus
- Verbs followed by the genitive

Materials
- Students' Book page 108
- Grammar Workbook page 16

1 Students read the text and translate the text in italics.

Answers:
children whose home is not safe or who are neglected by their parents / in Freiburg, the number of these children in care has unfortunately risen this year / one cause of this increase / cases of neglected children / the people in charge of the general social services / are fully aware of this difficult situation / as however the parents of these children / they are not capable of bringing up their children responsibly / despite initial difficulties / during this so-called time out / young people whose parents can't cope with the problems of puberty

2 Students use the *Tipp* section and the words in brackets to translate the sentences into German.

Answers:

a *Sie erfreuten sich ihrer Kinder trotz ihres Alters.*
b *Er nahm sich seiner Mutter an, nachdem sie aus dem Krankenhaus kam.*
c *Sie bezichtigte ihren Mann der Untreue.*
d *Wir wurden eines Verbrechens beschuldigt, das wir nicht begangen hatten.*

3 Students imagine they are a journalist and must interview the head of a youth office about children in care. They write up their interview using as many verbs in the genitive as possible.

5 Rechtswesen und Verbrechen

Skills focus

- Using the anticipatory *es*

Materials

- Students' Book page 109

1 Students translate the sentences into German. They should use a dictionary for any phrases they don't know. They should then make a list of these phrases and learn them.

Answers:

a *Man hätte (es) verhindern können, dass der Verbrecher der Polizei entkam.*
b *Nach vielen Debatten setzte die Stadt es durch, dass eine große Anzahl an Überwachungskameras in der Stadtmitte und in anderen gefährdeten Gebieten installiert wurden.*
c *Einige Eltern können es nicht lassen, ihre Kinder zu schlagen.*
d *Nach monatelanger Therapie gab er (es) auf, Drogen zu nehmen.*
e *Sie hatte es satt, auf ihre jüngere Schwester aufzupassen, die immer Ärger mit der Polizei hatte.*

2 Students read the text and translate it into English.

Possible answer:

The manager of a scientific research advice bureau has been sentenced to more than three years in prison by the Hildesheim district court. He was accused of 61 cases of bribery. The accused is said to have passed on candidates who wanted to do a PHD to a law professor, paying him fees. Apparently the accused wasn't aware that making these payments was a punishable offence. However, the court did not believe this and sentenced him to imprisonment, although the defence had asked for an acquittal. The law professor also received a three-month prison sentence.

3 Students rewrite the sentences using the verbs in brackets.

Answers:

a *Das Gericht lehnte es ab, den Angeklagten freizusprechen.*
b *Der Angeklagte konnte es nicht lassen, promotionswillige Kandidaten an einen Jura-Professor weiterzuleiten und diesem dann Honorare zu zahlen.*
c *Die promotionswilligen Kandidaten hätten es dem Angeklagten gegönnt, eine höhere Strafe zu bekommen.*
d *Man hat es dem Jura-Professor angemerkt, dass er sich schuldig fühlte.*

4 Students read the quote and then write an essay saying to what extent they agree with it. They should try to use as many of the verbs from activity 3 as possible and should give reasons for their viewpoint.

6 Technik und die Zukunft

Grammar focus

- Negative conditional clauses
- Alternatives for *wenn*
- Phrases used instead of w*enn*

Materials

- Students' Book page 110
- CD 2, track 24
- Grammar Workbook page 58

1a Students listen to the recording *Einkaufen im Jahr 2020* and note down verbs in the conditional. They should list these conditional sentences.

Answers:

Wenn sie ***geahnt hätte****, wie voll es hier heute Nachmittag* ***sein würde, hätte*** *sie gleich heute Morgen einen Platz* ***reservieren lassen****.*

Denn ohne sie ***wäre*** *sie überhaupt nicht in den Supermarkt* ***hineingekommen****.*

*Dann **hätte** sie ihre Einkäufe erst morgen **erledigen können**.*
*Als Susanne gerade an den Regalen mit Wein und anderen alkoholischen Getränken vorbeigeht, **wäre** sie fast in ein junges Mädchens **gerannt**, das eine Flasche Kirschwasser in der Hand hatte.*

***Hätte** ein Lesegerät die Kundenkarte des Mädchens nicht **registriert**, **wäre** die Verkäuferin nicht darauf aufmerksam **gemacht worden** und das minderjährige Mädchen **wäre** nicht **erwischt worden**.*

p 110, activity 1a

Susanne Freitag sucht verzweifelt eine Parklücke auf dem Parkplatz ihres Supermarkts. Wenn sie geahnt hätte, wie voll es hier heute Nachmittag sein würde, hätte sie gleich heute Morgen einen Platz reservieren lassen. Aber da entdeckt sie doch noch eine Lücke. Nun kann's losgehen! Sie steckt ihre Kundenkarte, die mit einem so genannten RFID-Chip ausgestattet ist, in einen Einkaufswagen, der sie freundlich mit Namen begrüßt. Am Griff des Einkaufswagens ist ein Bildschirm angebracht, auf dem sofort ihre Einkaufsliste erscheint, die der Supermarkt aus ihren letzten Einkäufen zusammengestellt hat. Zum Glück hat sie heute ihre Kundenkarte nicht vergessen. Denn ohne sie wäre sie überhaupt nicht in den Supermarkt hineingekommen. Dann hätte sie ihre Einkäufe erst morgen erledigen können. Als Susanne gerade an den Regalen mit Wein und anderen alkoholischen Getränken vorbeigeht, wäre sie fast in ein junges Mädchens gerannt, das eine Flasche Kirschwasser in der Hand hatte. Bevor Susanne etwas sagen konnte, kommt schon eine Verkäuferin und nimmt ihr die Flasche weg. Hätte ein Lesegerät die Kundenkarte des Mädchens nicht registriert, wäre die Verkäuferin nicht darauf aufmerksam gemacht worden und das minderjährige Mädchen wäre nicht erwischt worden. (from: www.ard.de/ratgeber, ARD Special/der gläserne Mensch)

1b Students translate the conditional sentences into English.

Answers:

- **a** *If she had guessed how full it would be here this afternoon, she already would have reserved a place this morning.*
- **b** *For without it, she wouldn't have got into the supermarket.*
- **c** *Then she would only have been able to do her shopping tomorrow.*
- **d** *Just as Susanne was walking past the shelves with wine and other alcoholic drinks, she almost ran into a young girl holding a bottle of Kirsch.*
- **e** *If a reading device had not registered the girl's customer card, the shop assistant would not have been made aware of it and the girl, who was under age, would not have been caught.*

2 Students translate the sentences into German.

Answers:

- **a** *Hätte es härtere Strafen gegeben, wären die Verbrecher abgeschreckt worden.*
- **b** *Hätte sie das Verbrechen gestanden, wäre sie vielleicht einer Gefängnisstrafe entgangen.*
- **c** *Ohne regelmäßiges Laufen und Fitnesstraining wären die Polizisten nicht so fit.*
- **d** *Dieses Verbrechen wäre nicht passiert, wenn mehr Polizisten unterwegs gewesen wären.*

3 Students write between 250 and 400 words on the subject of technical developments. To what extent would they make life easier?

4 Students complete the sentences with the correct form of the conditional.

Answers:

- **a** *hätte, gehabt; wäre, gekommen*
- **b** *wäre, verboten; wären, gestorben*
- **c** *hättest, angerufen; wären, entkommen*

Tipp

A Students write a sentence for the three other phrases featured in the *Tipp* box .

7 Literatur, Film und die bildende Kunst

Grammar focus

- Attributive participal phrases

Materials

- Students' Book page 111

1 Students translate the sentences into English.

Answers:

- **a** *It was possible to rescue the boy who was running away from his pursuer.*
- **b** *The author who was suffering from various illnesses was able to complete his novel only with a lot of effort.*

c *Her book which had been published recently became a bestseller with children between 10 and 12 years of age.*
d *Do you know the 2001 film version of the musical?*
e *One isn't sure what to think of the Wim Wenders Film which is currently showing in all cinemas.*

2 Students complete the sentences with the attributive participal phrases in brackets.

Answers:
a *Das **auf dem Boden liegende Buch** habe ich schon zweimal gelesen.*
b *Daniel Kehlmann ist ein mit **mit vielen Preisen ausgezeichneter** zeitgenössischer Schriftsteller.*
c *Das Tagebuch der Anne Frank ist ein von **vielen Jugendlichen in der ganzen Welt gelesenes** Dokument über den Holocaust im Zweiten Weltkrieg.*
d *Hier kann man eine supermoderne, sich **im Norden der Stadt ausbreitende** Architekur bewundern.*
e *Der **nach Luft schnappende, durch den Wald laufende** Held des Abenteuerfilms war ein miserabler Schauspieler.*

3a Students read the English text.

3b Students use the Internet to try to find out which film it is about.

3c Students translate the text into German, without using relative clauses.

Answer:
Jan, Peter und Julie, drei unbekümmerte, in Berlin lebende junge Rebellen teilen unter anderem ihren Ärger über die ungleiche Verteilung materieller Güter in der Gesellschaft. Während Julie an Demonstrationen gegen die der Gesundheit von Kindern schadenden süßwarengeschäfter teilnimmt, beabsichtigen Jan und Peter, den in ihren luxuriösen Villen lebenden Superreichen eine Lektion zu erteilen, indem sie bei ihnen einbrechen, jedoch ohne etwas zu stehlen. Stattdessen drehen sie die Möbel um und hinterlassen Botschaften wie "Sie haben zu viel Geld" oder "Die fetten Jahre sind vorbei" mit der Unterschrift "Die Erziehungsberechtigten". Als Peter, Julies Freund ins Ausland geht, kommen Jan und Julie sich näher, und Jan erzählt ihr von seinen und Peters regelmäßig nachts stattfindenden Aktionen. Und Julie macht von da an begeistert mit. Eines Nachts werden sie bei einem Einbruch von dem unerwartet zurückkehrenden Besitzer überrascht, und die drei 'Erziehungsberechtigten' werden in die Entführung des Besitzers verwickelt.

4 Students describe their favourite film or book. They should use attributive participal phrases in their writing.

8 Deutschland heute

Grammar focus
- The *Zustandspassiv*

Materials
- Students' Book page 112

1 Students translate the sentences into German. They should think about which form of the passive to use.

Answers:
a *750 Tonnen Nahrungsmittel werden jeden Tag nach Westberlin geflogen.*
b *Obwohl die Stadt von den sowjetischen Alliierten umgeben ist, geben ihre Bürger nicht auf.*
c *Die Rede des Berliner Bürgermeisters, das Volk von Berlin nicht aufzugeben, ist in die ganze Welt übertragen worden.*
d *Nach vielen Verhandlungen zwischen den Alliierten wurde entschieden, die Blockade zu beenden.*
e *Um 0.01 Uhr am 12. Mai ist die Blockade der sowjetischen Besatzungsmächte zu Ende.*

2 Students read the text about the Berlin Blockade and translate all passive sentences into English. They add in brackets which type of the passive is being used each time.

3 Students imagine that they lived through the time of the airlift in West Berlin. They describe their experiences and their feelings and reactions in the form of diary entries.

9 Politik – Globale Probleme

Skills focus
- Ways of translating the gerund

Materials

- Students' Book page 113

1 Students look at the sentences and choose the best translation. In some cases, both translations are possible.

Answers:
a 1 or 2 **b** 1 **c** 2 **d** 2

2a Students read the text about a strike by Lufthansa.

2b Students answer the questions in English.

Answers:

a *By reducing the number of flights, passengers could be warned in advance and had enough time to book a different flight.*

b *By ensuring a pay rise of 7.4% and by ensuring that there were no job losses*

c *By accepting the demands of the unions more quickly, Lufthansa could have avoided having to deal with lots of disappointed customers.* Or *could have avoided the strike action.*

3 Students write 200–250 on the effectiveness of strike action.

Essay-writing skills

Researching a topic

Materials

- Students' Book page 114

1 Students read the five essay titles.

2 Students decide which topics the titles cover. They should use the words in the box for help in doing this.

3 For each topic, students think of two or three terms that they could research on the Internet.

4 Students start researching their essay.

5 Students start think about planning their essay in more detail.

Planning an essay

Materials

- Students' Book page 115

1 Students order the points according to their importance when planning an essay.

2 Students look at the two model plans and compare them. They then discuss with a partner which one they think is better and why.

3 Students choose a different title and write out a plan. They should discuss their plan with a partner and add any suggestions they may have to improve it.

Writing an introduction and a conclusion

Materials

- Students' Book page 116

A1 Students decide which of the phrases would be appropriate for either the introduction of a literary essay or for a factual essay, and which for both.

A2 Students choose a title from page 114 and write a short introduction. They should then swap their introduction with a partner's and comment on his/her introduction, taking into consideration the list of do's and don't's.

B1 Students read the phrases, which can be used to start a conclusion, and translate them into English.

Answers:

a *As this discussion has shown, ...*
b *In conclusion it can be said that ...*
c *When weighing up the advantages and disadvantages, it becomes obvious that ...*
d *To sum up, I would say that ...*
e *This analysis/essay has shown how ...*

B2 Students compare the two conclusions and decide which one is better and why.

The main body of the essay

Materials

- Students' Book page 118

A1 Students translate the linking phrases into English.

Answers:

a *On the one hand ... on the other hand*
b *In contrast with ...*
c *Nevertheless there is/are also ...*
d *But nevertheless ...*
e *In comparison with this, ...*
f *It is quite different with ...*
g *Similarly ...*

B1 Students read the essay paragraph and make a list of all the 'do's' found in the paragraph.

Improving your language

Materials

- Students' Book page 118

A1 Students find synonyms for the commonly used verbs.

Answers:

a *illustrieren, darstellen*
b *erwähnen, erzählen*
c *organisieren, planen*
d *bestehen aus..., setzt sich zusammen aus..., existieren*

e *überlegen, glauben*
f *beobachten, betrachten*

A2 Students find synonyms for the following over-used nouns and phrases.

Answers:
a *Jugendliche, specific term, e.g Politiker, Einwohner, Bewohner*
b *meiner Ansicht/Meinung/Auffassung nach*
c *Streitfage, Schwierigkeit, Dilemma*
d *es zeigt sich, dass,.... wird deutlich, dass...*

B1a Students read the words and phrases and add any others after checking their notes.

B1b Students sort the nouns according to the following areas:
- types of crime
- types of punishments
- synonyms for the term 'crime'
- others

B2 Students choose a topic from page 114 and produce a word family of all the key terms. They should use their notes and relevant texts for support.

C1 Students translate the sentences using the passive, the conditional and the subjunctive.

Answers:
a *Wenn unsere Gesellschaft im letzten Jahrzehnt rücksichtsvoller gewesen wäre würde dieses Dilemma heute nicht existieren.*
b *Wenn alle Kernkraftwerke geschlossen würden, wären Tausende arbeitslos.*
c *Er hätte eine neue Stelle/Arbeit finden können, wenn er sich mehr für seine Weiterbildung interessiert hätte.*
d *Der Film wurde im Jahr 2003 produziert und war nicht nur in Deutschland sondern auch in anderen europäischen Ländern erfolgreich/ein Erfolg.*

C2 Students complete the sentences using the correct conjunction from the box.

Answers:
a *obwohl*
b *Wenn*
c *indem*
d *Während, dass*

3 Students complete the sentences using the correct relative pronoun.

Answers:
a *Der Film von Hans Weingartner, in **dem** es um die Themen Individuum und Gesellschaft und Geld und Macht geht, heißt ‚Die fetten Jahre sind vorbei'.*
b *Die Zahlen stammen von einer Statistik, **die** ich sehr aufschlussreich fand.*
c *Der zehnjährige Junge, **den** die Polizei festnahm, stammte aus einer Familie, in **der** Gewalt zum Alltag gehörte.*

Checking your work

Materials

- Students' Book page 119

1 Students write out the sentences using the correct word order.

Answers:
a *Zwar benötigt die Hightechindustrie besser qualifizierte Arbeitskräfte, aber sicher ist, dass viele Arbeitsplätze wegfallen werden.*
b *Die Arbeitnehmer sollten dafür sorgen, dass die Menschen umgeschult werden.*
c *Politiker und Wissenschaftler sind sich nicht einig inwieweit Stammzellenforschung gesetzlich erlaubt sein sollte, und wo man die Grenze ziehen sollte.*

2 Students complete the sentences with the correct form of the verb in brackets.

Answers:
a *In einem Interview sagte die Schriftstellerin Cornelia Funke, dass sie immer ein Notizbuch bei sich **habe**.*
b *Kirsten Boie **wurde** im Jahr 2007 mit dem Jugendliteraturpreis **ausgezeichnet**.*
c *Im Ausland **ist** die Nachfrage nach deutscher Jugendliteratur **gestiegen**.*

3 Students complete the sentences using the definite/indefinite article in the correct case.

Answers:
a *Viele neue wissenschaftliche Beiträge haben ihre Wurzeln in **der** Kernforschung.*
b *Die Umweltforschung ist **der/ein** Bereich, in **dem** das Forschungszentrum schon vor Jahren erfolgreich war.*
c *Aus der Sicht **der** Forscher bedeutet die Regelung eine Einschränkung.*

4 Students complete the sentences giving the words in brackets the correct adjective endings.

Answers:
a *Das **deutsche** Stammzellgesetz setzt der Forschung sehr **enge** Grenzen.*

b *Der **größte** Autohersteller hat schon das erste Serienauto mit **elektronischem** Antrieb angekündigt.*
c ***Moderne** Industrieunternehmen benötigen eine **zuverlässige** Energieversorgung.*

5 Students translate the sentences into German, paying particular attention to the points mentioned.

Answers:
a *Der Präsident wurde von der unerwarteten Ankunft seiner Familie überrascht.*
b *Die Gewalt der jungen Leute schockierte die ganze Stadt.*
c *Fremdenfeindlichkeit ist leider immer noch ein Problem, das gelöst werden muss.*